access 2007

WITHDRAWN

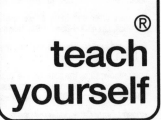

access 2007

moira stephen

for over 60 years, more than 50 million people have learnt over 750 subjects the **teach yourself** way, with impressive results.

be where you want to be with **teach yourself**

For UK order enquiries: please contact Bookpoint Ltd, 130 Milton Park, Abingdon, Oxon OX14 4SB. Telephone: +44 (0)1235 827720. Fax: +44 (0)1235 400454. Lines are open 09.00–17.00, Monday to Saturday, with a 24-hour message answering service. Details about our titles and how to order are available at www.teachyourself.co.uk.

For USA order enquiries: please contact McGraw-Hill Customer Services, PO Box 545, Blacklick, OH 43004-0545, USA. Telephone: 1-800-722-4726. Fax: 1-614-755-5645.

For Canada order enquiries: please contact McGraw-Hill Ryerson Ltd, 300 Water St, Whitby, Ontario L1N 9B6, Canada. Telephone: 905 430 5000. Fax: 905 430 5020.

Long renowned as the authoritative source for self-guided learning – with more than 50 million copies sold worldwide – the **teach yourself** series includes over 500 titles in the fields of languages, crafts, hobbies, business, computing and education.

British Library Cataloguing in Publication Data: a catalogue record for this title is available from The British Library.

Library of Congress Catalog Card Number: on file.

First published in UK 2007 by Hodder Education, 338 Euston Road, London NW1 3BH.

First published in USA 2007 by The McGraw-Hill Companies Inc.

The **teach yourself** name is a registered trademark of Hodder Headline.

Computer hardware and software brand names mentioned in this book are protected by their respective trademarks and are acknowledged.

The publisher has used its best endeavours to ensure that the URLs for external websites referred to in this book are correct and active at the time of going to press. However, the publisher has no responsibility for the websites and can give no guarantee that a site will remain live or that the content is or will remain appropriate.

 Typeset by MacDesign, Southampton

Printed in Great Britain for Hodder Education, a division of Hodder Headline, 338 Euston Road, London NW1 3BH, by Cox & Wyman Ltd, Reading, Berkshire.

Hodder Headline's policy is to use papers that are natural, renewable and recyclable products and made from wood grown in sustainable forests. The logging and manufacturing processes are expected to conform to the environmental regulations of the country of origin.

Impression number   10 9 8 7 6 5 4 3 2 1

Year   2011 2010 2009 2008 2007

contents

Welcome to *Teach Yourself Access*.

This book is for the user who wants to be able to harness the power of Access *without* being overpowered by jargon. Whether you have never used a database in your life, or are familiar with databases but new to Access, this book will have you up and running quickly on this very popular package.

Teach Yourself Access takes you through the main processes of building and using efficient Access databases. You can work through from beginning to end (recommended for new users) or dip into a chapter and apply the techniques to your own database. Over the course of the book we will cover:

* **Database design:** What do you want from your database? What data will you need to store? How can you organize your data efficiently in a database?

* **Jargon and concepts:** Databases and their technology are explained in layman's terms – not computer-speak!

* **Essential database skills:** Setting up table structures, entering and editing data and extracting information from your database are all explored.

* **Ease of use:** Whether you are designing a database for your own use, or one for others to use, the interface between the user and the data is very important. You will find out how to design friendly 'front-ends' for your databases, so that once a database is set up, it is easy to use.

* **Efficient working practices:** Macros are introduced to give you an insight into how they can help you become more efficient as you use Access.

This book aims to be a useful learning aid, whether you are working by yourself or teaching others in a classroom, and the project that it contains should make ideal teaching material.

I hope you enjoy using this book and find it useful when learning to use Access and wish you success in working with databases.

Moira Stephen

2007

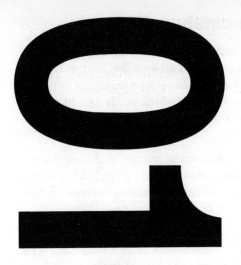

01

getting started

In this chapter you will learn:

- basic database concepts
- what you need to run Access 2007
- how to install the software
- how to start Access
- about the Access screen
- how to use the Help system

1.1 What is a database?

A database is simply a collection of data. For example, it may be your Christmas card name and address list, or details about books, CDs and videos in your library or it may be company data (with details of customers, suppliers, products sold, orders, employees). The data is collected and organized for a particular purpose.

Most modern database management systems (including Access) use the relational database management model. This simply means that all the data stored in the database is related to one subject, e.g. your company, or the items in your library.

In a simple database, it may be feasible to store all the information together in one **table** (see section 1.2 for a definition) – for instance, a Christmas card name and address list. Other databases are more complex – your library or company database for example. The data would then need to be divided up into several tables, which could be linked as and when required. Data about two classes of information (such as 'books' and 'publishers' in a library situation) can be manipulated as a single entry based on related data values.

For example, in your library you might want to store specific details on each book – title, author, category, ISBN, number held, year published, publisher, etc. – on your system. It would be very repetitive (and pointless) to store all the name, address and other contact details for the publisher with each book detail, since you may have the same detail duplicated hundreds of times, if one publisher is responsible for many of your books.

Therefore, in a relational system, when you store information about a book, you include a data field that can be used to connect each book with its publisher details, e.g. *Publisher Code*. The publisher details would then be stored in a separate table. The name, address and contact details of each publisher would only need to be recorded once, and could be linked to any book through the *Publisher Code* field whenever necessary.

1.2 Database jargon

Some database terminology may be unfamiliar to you. Below you will find brief definitions of the terms you are likely to meet in the near future. Don't worry about trying to understand them all at once – things become clearer as you use Access.

Table

In a relational database, all the data on one topic is stored in a table. If your database requirements are fairly simple, you might have only one table in your database. If your requirements are more complex, your database may contain several tables. In the Library database example, you could have a table for your book data, one for publisher data and perhaps one for author data.

The data in the table is structured in a way that will allow you to get information from it – 'interrogate it' – conveniently. All of the data on one item, e.g. a book or a publisher, is held in the record for that book or publisher, within the appropriate table.

Record

A record contains information about a single item in your table. All the detail relating to one book will be held in that book's record in the Book table. Information about a publisher will be held in a record for that publisher in the Publisher table. The record is broken down into several **fields** – one for each piece of detail about your item (book, publisher, etc.).

Field

A field is a piece of data within a record. In your book's record, things like book title, author-firstname, author-surname, category, number held, library code, location, ISBN, publisher code, etc. would all be held in separate fields. In a publisher record, you would have fields for name, address (perhaps separate fields for street, town, postcode, county), telephone number, fax number, e-mail address, etc.

Each field has a name that identifies it.

Relationship

This determines the way in which the detail in one table is related to the detail in another table, e.g. through the publisher code. Publishers would have a one-to-many relationship with books as one publisher could have published many books.

Join

The process of linking tables or queries.

Data definition

The process of defining what data will be stored in your database, specifying the data field's type (it might be numbers or characters), the data field's size and indicating how it is related to data in other tables.

Data manipulation

Once your data is set up, you can work with it in many ways. This may involve sorting it into a specific order, or extracting specific records from tables, or listing detail from a number of different tables into one report.

1.3 Schematic diagram

The diagram opposite illustrates a simple database. The Book table would be related to the Publisher table through the publisher code field. The Book table has been expanded to indicate what fields might be included in it. In the example, the Author table could be related to both the Publisher table and the Book table.

* Each record in a table is presented in a row – in this example each book is a record.

* Each field in a table is in a column – there is a Title field, Author field, etc.

* Each field has a field name at the top of the column: Title, Author, Category.

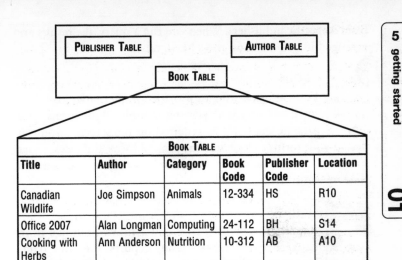

BOOK TABLE					
Title	Author	Category	Book Code	Publisher Code	Location
Canadian Wildlife	Joe Simpson	Animals	12-334	HS	R10
Office 2007	Alan Longman	Computing	24-112	BH	S14
Cooking with Herbs	Ann Anderson	Nutrition	10-312	AB	A10
Hiking in Iceland	Thomas Allan	Travel	20-100	XY	B17

Example of a library database

1.4 Access objects

An Access database consists of objects that can be used to input, display, interrogate, print and automate your work. They are displayed in the Navigation pane. The purpose of each object is summarized below.

Tables

Tables are the most important objects in your database. Tables are used for data entry and editing.

In a table, each record is displayed as a row and each field is displayed as a column. You can display a number of records on the screen at any one time, and as many fields as will fit on your screen. Any records or fields not displayed can be scrolled into view as required.

Queries

You use queries to locate specific records within your tables. You might want to extract records that meet selection criteria (e.g. all children's books, or books from a specific publisher). When you run a query, the results are arranged in columns and rows like a table.

Forms

You can use forms to provide an alternative to tables for data entry and viewing records. With forms, you arrange the fields as required on the screen – you can design your forms to look like the printed forms (invoices, order forms, etc.) that you use. A form displays only one record at a time on the screen.

Reports

Reports can be used to produce printed outputs from data in your database. Using reports, the same database can produce, for instance, a list of one publisher's books, a set of mailing labels for letters, or a report on books in a specific category.

Macros

Macros are used to automate the way you use Access, and can be used to build some very sophisticated applications. They are introduced at the end of this book.

1.5 System requirements

The hardware and software specifications given are for Office 2007. The recommended configuration is a PC with a minimum of a 500 MHz processor, 256 MB of RAM and 1.5 GB disk space. The minimum specification is given in the table opposite.

See http://www.microsoft.com for full details of system requirements.

Access is present in four of the Office 2007 suite editions: Professional, Professional Plus, Enterprise and Ultimate. For full details of what is included in each edition visit http://www.microsoft.com.

Processor	500 MHz or higher
Memory	256 MB RAM or higher
Hard disk	1.5 GB. A portion of this will be freed after installation if the installation files are removed from the hard drive.
Drive	CD-ROM or DVD drive
Display	1024 × 768 or higher resolution monitor
Operating system	Windows XP with Service Pack 2, Windows Server with Service Pack 1, or later system.
Other	Certain features, e.g. inking, speech recognition, Information Rights Management have specific requirements – check out the Microsoft website.
Browser	Internet Explorer 6.0 or later, 32-bit browser only.

Hardware and software requirements for Access 2007.

1.6 Installing Access

To install Microsoft Office, follow the on-screen instructions:

1 Insert the CD into the CD drive.

◆ The CD will launch automatically, and the setup begin.

2 At the Setup dialog box, enter the 25-character product key.

3 For the user information, enter your name, initials (optional) and organization (optional).

◆ Your name will be used in the Author box in the Properties dialog box in the Office programs.

4 Read the End-User License Agreement and select *I accept the terms* (if you don't agree, you can't continue).

5 Select the type of installation.

6 At the final Setup stage, select the options and you're done!

Entering your product key at installation helps to verify that your software is legitimate. You will be able to run your 2007 Microsoft Office system programs up to 25 times before you have to enter the key – after this the software goes into Reduced Functionality mode and many features will be unavailable.

1.7 Preparing your data

The most important (and often most difficult) stage in setting up any database takes place away from the computer. Before you set up a database you must get your data organized.

There are two key questions that need to be addressed:

* What do you want to store?

* What information do you want to get out of the database?

Take your time and work out your answers before you start.

Once you have decided what you are storing, and what use you intend to make of the data, you are ready to start designing the database. Much of this can be done away from the computer.

What fields do you need?

You must break down the data into the smallest units (fields) that you will want to store, search or sort on.

If you are setting up names, you would probably break the name into three fields – *Title*, *First name* (or *Initials*) and *Surname*. This way you can sort the file into *Surname* order, or search for someone using the *First name* and *Surname*.

If you are storing addresses, you would probably want separate fields for *Town/city*, *County* and/or *Country*. You can then sort your records into order on any of these fields, or locate records by specifying appropriate search criteria. For example, using *Town/city* and *Country* fields, you could search for addresses in Washington (*Town/city*), USA (*Country*) rather than Washington (*Town/city*), UK (*Country*).

Organize!

This is very important! Organize your data before you start. Decide what you want to store, what you want to do with it, and what fields are required (for sorting and searching). It will save you a lot of time and frustration in the long run!

When planning your database, take a small sample of the data you wish to store and examine it carefully. This will help you confirm what fields will be required.

How big are the fields?

You must also decide how much space is required for each field. The space you allocate must be long enough to accommodate the longest item that might go there. How long is the longest surname you want to store? If in doubt, take a sample of some typical names (Anderson, Johnston, Mackenzie, Harvey-Jones?) and add a few more characters to the longest one to be sure. An error in field size isn't as serious as an error in record structure as field can be expanded without existing data being affected.

You can edit the structure of your table if necessary – but hunting through existing data to update records is time consuming, so it is best to get it right to start with!

1.8 Normalization of data

As well as deciding what you need to store, you also want to minimize any data duplication as far as possible. For example, in the library scenario you may want to keep a record of the name, address and contact details of the publishing company for each book you hold. You could keep this information in the same table as the book detail as illustrated on the next page.

Title	Author	Category	Library code	Number held	Publisher	Publisher address	Publisher telephone number

We have already touched upon the fact that this approach could present some basic problems, the most obvious ones being:

- **Effort to maintain your data** – keeping the data up to date could result in a lot of work as the same publisher fields are in many book records. A change in the telephone number of a publisher would result in many fields having to be updated.

- **Size** – your database would end up much larger than necessary because all of the publisher detail would be repeated many times.

- **Accuracy** – having to key the same detail in several times can easily lead to errors.

The solution to this kind of problem is to use a process called *normalization*. As a result of normalization, you end up organizing your data fields into a group of tables, which can easily be linked when and as required.

The simple solution to this problem is to create two tables – one for the book detail, and one for the publisher detail. In each table you would need a Publisher ID (or Publisher Code) field, that would be used to identify each publisher uniquely. This field could then be used to link the tables when and as required.

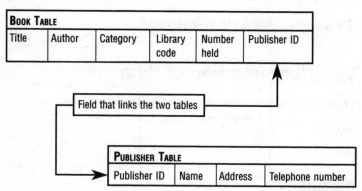

There are several benefits to this approach:

- Each set of publisher details is stored (and therefore keyed in) once only.

- The Book table will be considerably smaller in size than it otherwise would have been.

- Should any of the publisher details change (e.g. phone number) you only have one record to update (in the Publisher table).

- If you wrongly identify a publisher in a record in the Book table, you have one field only to correct, rather than all of the publisher's fields.

1.9 Starting Access

1 Click the **Start** button on the Taskbar.

2 Point to **All Programs**.

3 Select **Microsoft Office**.

4 Click **Microsoft Office Access 2007**.

The Getting Started window is displayed on your screen.

This window is divided into four main areas:

* Template categories on the left.

* New database options in the upper part of the middle area.

* Links to Office Online in the lower part of the middle.

* A list of recently-used databases on the right, with a **More** command so that you can locate other databases.

Templates   New database   Recently-used databases

Office Online links

More

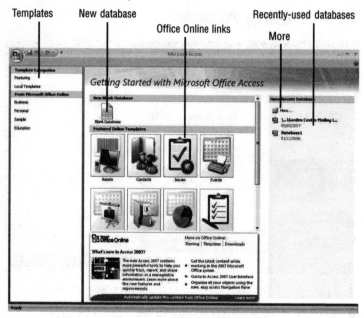

1.10 Create a blank database

We will look at the various options shortly, but in the meantime we will create a new blank database so that we can have a look at the Access screen.

To create a new blank database:

1 Click **Blank Database** under the **New Blank Database** heading.

Blank Database

To store your database in the suggested location:

2 Give your database a name.

3 Click **Create**.

Or

Blank Database

Create a Microsoft Office Access database that does not contain any existing data or objects.

File Name:

My First Database.accdb

C:\Documents and Settings\All Users\Documents\Moira\Books\2007 Access\

Create   Cancel

To select a different location for your file:

4 Click **Browse** .

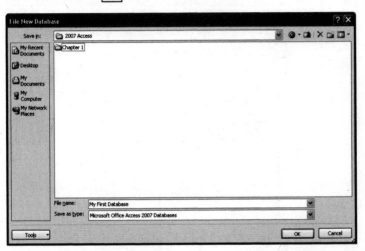

5 Specify a drive/folder for your file in the **Save in** field.

6 Enter a name for the database in the **File name** field.

7 Leave the **Save as Type** at *Microsoft Office Access 2007 Databases*.

8 Click **OK** to close the **File New Database** dialog box.

9 Click **Create**.

• Your database will be created and will be displayed in Datasheet view.

1.11 The Access screen

We'll take a tour of the Access screen, so that you know what the various areas are called. You'll find the screen areas referred to by these names in the online Help, throughout this book and in other publications on the package.

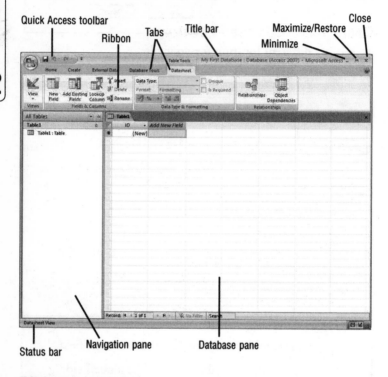

Quick Access toolbar

Ribbon

Tabs

Title bar

Minimize

Maximize/Restore

Close

Status bar

Navigation pane

Database pane

Ribbon and tabs

The Access features and commands are displayed on the Ribbon along the top of the database. The Ribbon is divided into task-orientated tabs, where the commands required for different tasks are grouped, e.g. the Create tab has the objects you can create.

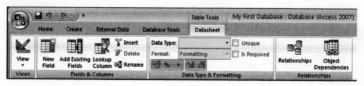

- To toggle the display of the Ribbon, press [Ctrl]-[F1].

- To temporarily display any tab when the Ribbon is hidden, click on a tab.

Program tabs replace the standard tabs when you perform certain tasks, e.g. Print Preview.

Groups and command buttons

The buttons on each tab are arranged in groups, e.g. the Datasheet tab has the buttons grouped together into areas – Views, Fields & Columns, Data Type & Formatting and Relationships.

The Microsoft Office button

The Microsoft Office button is located at the top left of the Access screen. When clicked it displays a menu that gives you access to all the things you can do with your file, e.g. print, save, open, send by e-mail.

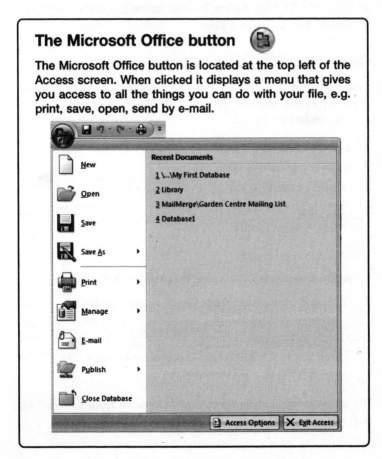

1.12 Quick Access toolbar

The Quick Access toolbar contains commands that are used regularly, and are independent from the tab being displayed. The toolbar can be displayed in one of two positions:

* Above the Ribbon, by the Microsoft Office button (default position).

* Below the Ribbon.

To move it from one position to the other:

1 Click the down arrow at the right of the Quick Access toolbar.

2 Click **Place Quick Access Toolbar below the Ribbon** or **Place Quick Access Toolbar above the Ribbon** as required.

Customizing the Quick Access toolbar

You may find it useful to add other commands that you use regularly to this toolbar, e.g. open file, new file. You can easily add or remove tools.

To add a command:

1 Right-click on the command you want to add.

2 Left-click on **Add to Quick Access Toolbar...**

To remove a command:

1 Right-click on the command that you wish to remove.

2 Left-click on **Remove from Quick Access Toolbar...**

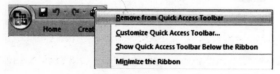

If you have several buttons to add or remove from the toolbar, you could do so from the **Access Options** dialog box.

To display the Customize options:

1 Right-click on the Microsoft Office button.

2 Left-click on **Customize Quick Access Toolbar...**

<u>R</u>emove from Quick Access Toolbar
<u>C</u>ustomize Quick Access Toolbar...
<u>S</u>how Quick Access Toolbar Below the Ribbon
Mi<u>n</u>imize the Ribbon

3 Explore the **Access Options, Customize** area and add or remove tools as required.

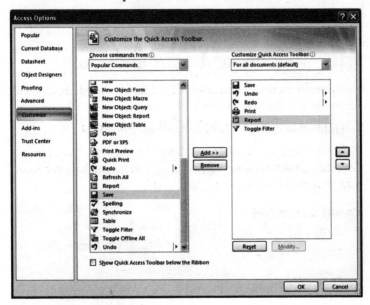

To add a command:

• Select it in the list on the left and click **Add>>**.

To remove a command:

• Select it in the list on the right and click **Remove**.

To change the position of the commands on the toolbar:

• Select a command in the right-hand list and click the up or down arrow to the right of this list.

To reset the toolbar to its original settings:

• Click **Reset** and confirm at the prompt.

Dialog box launcher

Dialog Box launchers are small buttons that appear at the bottom right of some groups. Clicking the launcher opens a dialog box that displays more options related to the group.

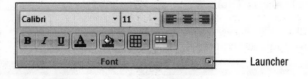

Launcher

1.13 Ribbon keyboard shortcuts

If you prefer to issue commands using the keyboard, Access will automatically prompt you as you work.

1 Hold down [Alt] – and keep it down throughout the procedure.

2 A ghost letter appears next to each tab on the Ribbon. Press the letter on your keyboard to activate the tab you want.

♦ Ghost letters/numbers will appear next to each command.

3 Press the letter/number to select the command required.

4 Release [Alt].

1.14 Navigation pane

The Navigation pane is displayed on the left of the screen in Datasheet view. The Navigation pane replaces the Database window in Access 2007. This pane will display a list of the tables, queries, forms and reports in your database.

You can hide and display this pane by clicking the Shutter button at its top right. When collapsed, the pane becomes a narrow column at the left of the screen.

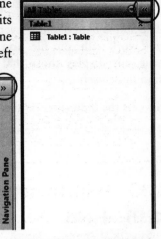

• Click the Shutter button at the top of the column to restore the pane.

You can change the way in which your database objects are grouped in the Navigation pane. The display that most resembles previous versions is **By Object Type**. This displays objects in the groups Tables, Queries, Forms and Reports.

You can change the display from the Navigation pane menu. To open this, click the menu bar at the top of the pane.

You can filter the objects using the menu, e.g. by Object type.

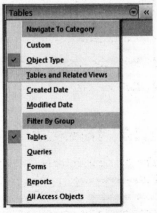

If you choose **Tables and Related Views**, all the queries, forms and reports associated with a table are grouped together.

Experiment with the Navigation pane as your database develops – we will revisit it in Chapter 11.

1.15 Status bar configuration

The Status bar contains several status indicators to help you as you work with your file. You can add and remove these, so that you only display those that you find most useful.

To edit the indicators on the bar:

1 Right-click on the Status bar.

2 Select or deselect the indicator as required.

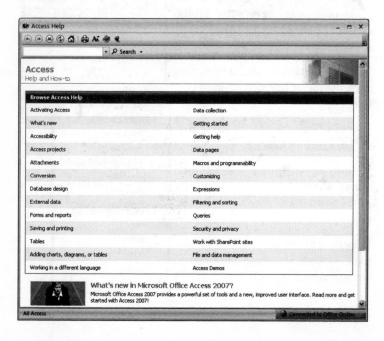

Customize Status Bar	
✓ Caps Lock	Off
✓ Kana Mode	
✓ Num Lock	Off
✓ Scroll Lock	Off
Overtype	
✓ Filtered	
✓ Move Mode	
✓ Extended Selection	
✓ View Shortcuts	

1.16 Help

As you work with Access you may find that you come a bit unstuck from time to time and need help. If you are offline, Access will use the Help system installed on your PC; if you are online you will also have access to all the Help on the Microsoft website.

Access Help

Search

Access
Help and How-to

Browse Access Help	
Activating Access	Data collection
What's new	Getting started
Accessibility	Getting help
Access projects	Data pages
Attachments	Macros and programmability
Conversion	Customizing
Database design	Expressions
External data	Filtering and sorting
Forms and reports	Queries
Saving and printing	Security and privacy
Tables	Work with SharePoint sites
Adding charts, diagrams, or tables	File and data management
Working in a different language	Access Demos

What's new in Microsoft Office Access 2007?
Microsoft Office Access 2007 provides a powerful set of tools and a new, improved user interface. Read more and get started with Access 2007!

All Access   Connected to Office Online

To access the Help system:

• Click the **Help** button to the right of the Ribbon or press **[F1]**.

Browse through the Help pages to get an idea of the Help that is available. You'll find everything from Help pages that will guide the beginner through getting started, to Help on some of the more sophisticated querying and reporting features.

The Help toolbar

Use the Help toolbar as you work in the Help pages.

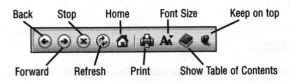

Back   Stop   Home   Font Size   Keep on top

Forward   Refresh   Print   Show Table of Contents

To search for Help:

1 Type what you are looking for in the **Search** field.

2 Click **Search**.

Or

• Click the search drop-down arrow and select a search area.

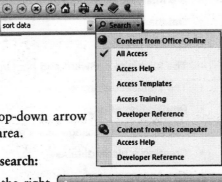

To return to an earlier search:

• Click the arrow to the right of the Search field and select the topic you wish to revisit.

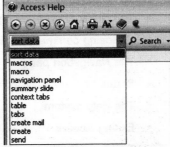

1.17 Exiting Access

When you have finished working in Access you must close the application down – don't just switch off your computer.

To exit Access:

• Click the Microsoft Office button then **Exit Access** at the bottom right of the menu.

Or

• Click the **Close** button in the right-hand corner of the application title bar.

Summary

This chapter has introduced you to Access 2007. We have discussed:

• **What a database is and what it might be used for (there are many other examples throughout the book)**

• **Database jargon**

• **Access Objects**

• **The minimum software and hardware requirements**

• **The installation procedure**

• **Preparation of data**

• **Accessing the package using the Start menu**

• **Creating a blank database**

• **The Access screen**

• **The Quick Access toolbar**

• **Choosing commands using the keyboard**

• **The Navigation pane**

• **Status bar configuration**

• **The Help system**

• **Exiting Access.**

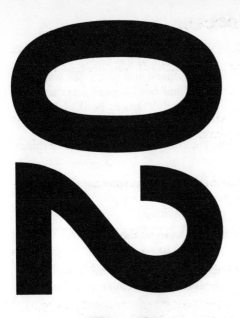

02

database design

In this chapter you will learn:

- how to start planning your database
- about data normalization
- about table relationships
- how to create a database
- how to open and close a database

2.1 The project

The main project in this book is the setting up of a library database. The database will contain details of the books we have on our shelves, the authors, the publishers, and so on. We will limit the scope of the project to handling books, publishers and authors – library members' details and details of books borrowed will not be included at this stage.

Before you start working on the computer, there are three things you should do:

- Draw up a list of what is required from your database. Work out what you want to be able to do with your database. What tasks do you want to perform with it?

- Identify the fields required. Analyse the tasks and identify the data items (fields) you need to set up.

- Normalize your data to minimize redundant data – data that is duplicated unnecessarily can cause problems (see section 1.8).

2.2 Draw up a list of requirements

The first thing you must do is sit down and think! Before you start to do anything on the computer, work out what it is that you intend to do with your database. Make a list of all the things you want your database to be able to provide for you. What information do you want to record? What kind of questions will you want the system to provide answers to? What reports do you want to generate?

Using our Library database example, we might come up with the following list of things we would like to be able to do:

- Record, update and edit details of all the books held in the library – title, author, publisher, etc.

- Keep details of the different categories of book held, e.g. science, travel, cooking.

- Hold publisher details – name, address, telephone number, etc.

- Give the physical location of the book in the library – row, shelf number, etc.

- Provide details about the author of the book.

- Extract different sets of data, e.g.:
  - a list of all travel books from a specific publisher
  - a list of science and astronomy books by a given author.
- Prepare and print reports on various things:
  - details of books in specific categories
  - lists of books from a given publisher
  - lists of books by a particular author.

Once you have established what you want to be able to do with your database, you can start to plan how it might best be set up.

There are several things to consider here. In our example we want to record details of the books, publishers and authors of the books in our library. We want to be able to work with the data easily, without all the staff needing to become computer 'whizz kids' and we want to be able to extract selective details from our database and print out attractive reports! Sounds good!

2.3   Identify the detail required

You must now work out what detail you will need to store to enable your Access database to fulfil the requirements you have identified for it. Make a list of the tasks you want your database to perform.

Then consider each task individually, and write down what data items you think you will need for that task. A data item is simply a single piece of information about the thing you are working with – the book, author or publisher in our case. Include any notes that may be useful as you are working on your design. It is usually easy to think of the first few things you need, then it becomes harder as the list gets longer.

Write down the data items you come up with, and edit the list as you go through the process.

The use of a simple form can be handy here. In the next two pages are suggestions of what might be necessary for the list of requirements we have identified for the Library database.

Task 1: Record, update and edit details of all books held in the library – title, author, publisher, etc.

Detail	Description	Notes
ISBN	Unique reference	Primary Key (see page 29)
Title	Book title	
Author	Personal details	Name, date of birth, date of death, nationality, specialist area, any other information The information would be best held in a separate table, linked to the book table through the AuthorID. This approach would reduce unnecessary duplication of detail (which should mean a smaller database, with fewer errors).
Publisher	Contact details	Name, address, phone number, fax number, e-mail address, website The information would be best held in a separate table, linked to the book table through the PublisherID. This approach would reduce unnecessary duplication of detail and help promote accuracy.
Category	e.g. Science, History, Music, Cookery	The categories could be held in a separate Categories table and detail would be 'looked up' from the book table
Location	Row and shelf number	
Copies	Number held	
Pub. Year		
Price		
Reference or Lending	Identifies reference or lending book	

Task 2: Keep details of the different categories of book we hold, e.g. science, travel, cooking

Detail	Description	Notes
Category name	Unique description of category	e.g. Science, History, Travel

Task 3: Hold publisher details – name, address, telephone number, etc.

Detail	Description	Notes
PublisherID	Unique identifier for each	Primary Key
Publisher Name		
Publisher Address		
Publisher Phone Number		
Publisher Fax		
Publisher e-mail address		

Task 4: Give the physical location of the book in the library – row, shelf number, etc.

Detail	Description	Notes
Row Number ID		
Shelf ID		

Task 5: Provide details about the author of the book

Detail	Description	Notes
AuthorID	Unique identifier for each	Primary Key
Surname		
Firstname		
Date of Birth		
Date of Death		
Nationality		
Speciality		
Notes		

Task 6: Extract different sorts of data from your database

- Ensure that table structure is broken down into the fields you want to sort and select on.

- Try to think of all the questions you might want to ask of your data, and set up the fields required when you specify the table structures. For example, if you want to be able to find out from your data the titles of all the books you hold by a particular author, together with the publisher name and the year of publication, you will need to have a *Book Title* field, an *Author Name* field, a *Publisher* field and *Year Published* field somewhere in your database.

♦ Relational database structures are easy to edit, so it is possible to add, delete or edit fields that you make an error in at the setup stage. However, a bit of forward thinking at this stage can minimize the number of amendments that you will need to make in the future.

Task 7: Prepare and print reports on various things

♦ Ensure that table structure includes the fields required for the reports.

♦ Areas to consider here are as per the notes in the previous task.

♦ If you want to be able to produce a report grouping the books you hold under the heading *Publisher*, perhaps with an author grouping within the publisher grouping, the book titles sorted in ascending alphabetical order, and the total number of books held from each publisher displayed, you must have the fields required set up in the structure of your tables.

We also want to make the database easy to use. To facilitate this we could:

♦ Include validation checks on data to help reduce errors.

♦ Design a user-friendly interface for staff.

Once you have completed this stage of the planning process, you can work out what fields will be required, how best to group the fields into tables and how the tables will be related to each other.

2.4 Normalization

When deciding on the tables required, you should consider how best to group the fields to minimize the duplication of data throughout the database – this is what is meant by the process of *normalization*.

Table structure

Using the information contained in the lists above, we might decide to record all the Book details in one table, but use a separate table for the Publisher detail and a separate table for the Author detail. We could also have a fourth table that contains a list of the different categories of book. You must decide which fields should be in each table.

You must also decide what kind of data will be held in each field – will it be text, numbers, date, currency and so on?

Primary key

You should identify a field (or combination of fields) that would uniquely identify each record held within each table. This field (or group of fields) would be the *primary key* for the table. In our example a single field in each table would be sufficient for the primary key.

In the *Book* table the *ISBN* would be different for each book, so this would make the ideal primary key for the *Book* table. Each publisher would have their own ID, so this would be the field to choose for the primary key, and each author would have their own ID, so the *AuthorID* would be the field to choose for the primary key in the *Author* table.

By breaking the detail down into four tables in this way, the details on each publisher would need to be recorded only once, in the *Publisher* table. The details on each author would also need to be recorded only once, in the *Author* table. The *Category* names would need to be entered only once. Within the *Book* table, you would simply need to enter the publisher, author and category codes in the appropriate fields and these would facilitate the link through to the other tables when required.

Details of the book's location within the library could be held in the main book table – there is no real benefit to be derived from placing this in a separate table.

The field lists, showing their names, possible data types and notes, for the four tables are given on the following pages. The use of data types should be fairly obvious, but look ahead to Chapter 3 if you want to know more about any of them at this point.

Book table

The field list for the *Book* table would be:

Book Table		
Field Name	**Data Type**	**Notes**
ISBN	Text	Primary key
Title	Text	
AuthorID	Number	
PublisherID	Number	
Category	Text	Look up Category Name field
Row Number	Number	
Shelf Number	Number	
Number of Copies	Number	
Publication Year	Number	Year only held
Price	Currency	
Reference or Lending	Text	

Publisher table

The field list for the *Publisher* table (with data types) would be:

Publisher Table		
Field Name	**Data Type**	**Notes**
PublisherID	AutoNumber *	Primary Key
Company	Text	
Address 1	Text	Size = 25
Address 2	Text	Size = 25
City	Text	Size = 30
Postcode	Text	Size = 14
Region	Text	Size = 30
Country	Text	Size = 20
Business Phone	Text	Size = 30
Fax Number	Text	Size = 30
E-mail address	Text	Size = 40
Website	Hyperlink	

Author table

The field list for the *Author* table (with data types) would be:

Author Table		
Field Name	**Data Type**	**Notes**
AuthorID	AutoNumber	Primary key
Surname	Text	
Firstname	Text	
Date of Birth	Date	
Date of Death	Date	
Nationality	Text	
Speciality	Text	
Notes	Text	

Category table

We can use another table to identify the category of book. By doing this, the full name of the book category would need to be keyed in only once, but it could be 'looked up' from the *Book* table at any time using a 'Look Up' option.

Category Table		
Field Name	**Data Type**	**Notes**
Category name	Text	Primary key

So, by using some forward planning, we have reached the stage where we have decided that a database consisting of four tables is just what we need for this situation.

2.5 Relationships

The *Book* table in our database is related to each of the other tables within the database as indicated below.

Table	Related to	Joining Fields	Type of Relationship
Publisher	Book	PublisherID	One-to-many
Author	Book	AuthorID	One-to-many
Category	Book	Category Name	One-to-many

The type of relationship in each case is one-to-many (this is the most common type of relationship between tables). One record in the *Publisher* table may be related to many records in the *Book* table – our library contains lots of books from each publisher. One record in the *Author* table may be related to many records in the *Book* table – many authors have written more than one book. One record in the *Category* table may be related to many records in the *Book* table – there are many books in each of our book categories. The tables are related to each other as shown in this diagram.

The lines between the tables indicate which fields are related to each other – these are called **join lines** in Access.

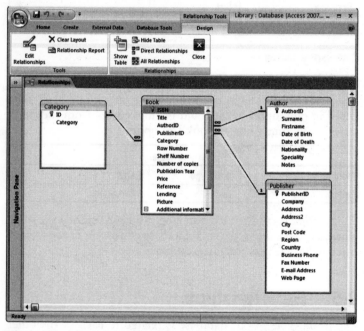

The primary key in each table is shown in bold – the relationships we need are between the primary key of the *Author*, *Publisher* and *Category* tables and the appropriate **foreign key** (the **primary key** viewed from another table) in the *Book* table.

You will learn how to define the table structures and set the relationships in Chapter 3.

2.6 Create a new database

If necessary, start Access and create a new blank database called Library. If Access is already running, create a new database.

To create a new blank database:

1 Click the Microsoft Office button and select **New**.

2 Follow the instructions in section 1.10.

2.7 Open a database file

If you have closed your Library database you should open it again. If you are launching Access, you can open a recently used file from the Open list on the Getting Started screen.

If Access is already running, you can open your database from the Microsoft Office button menu.

To open your database:

1 Click the Microsoft Office button and select your file from the Recent Document list.

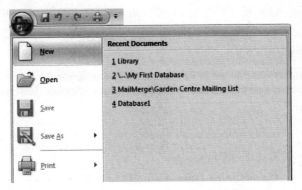

Or

2 Click **Open** on the Office button menu or use the keyboard shortcut [**Ctrl**]-[**O**].

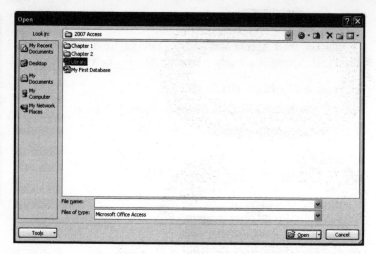

3 Locate your database in the **Open** dialog box.

4 Select and open your file.

2.8 Close file

+ To close your file, click the Microsoft Office button and choose **Close** from the menu.

Or

+ Click the Close button at the top right of the Access window.

Summary

In this chapter we have introduced the groundwork required before you start to set up the tables in your Access database:

+ Drawing up a list of requirements

+ Requirements analysis and field identification

+ Normalization of data

+ Relationships between tables

+ Creating a new database file

+ Opening an existing database file.

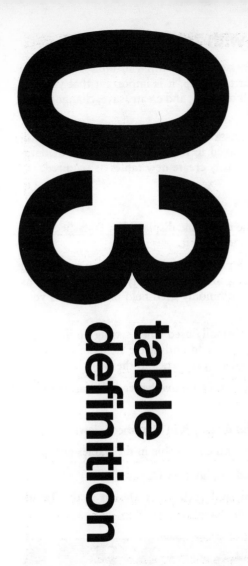

03
table definition

In this chapter you will learn:

- how to create a table
- about the different data types and their properties
- how to set up a table using a table template

3.1 Working with tables

The data in your database will be stored in tables. Before we actually start to set our tables up, it is important that you can use the basic table handling skills, and create, save, change views, close and open tables.

When you create a new database, a new table is produced automatically, and it is displayed in Datasheet view. As your database develops, you can easily create new tables as required.

Create a new table

You can opt to have the new table displayed in Datasheet view or Design view when you create it.

Datasheet view is used for data entry and editing purposes. You can also add new fields and specify data types in this view as well as assign the most commonly-used field properties to your field.

Design view is the one normally used when setting up the structure of your table. You can add and delete fields in this view, specify data types and assign properties to the fields.

Once a table is created, you can move between Datasheet view and Design view at any time.

To create your table and display it in Datasheet view:

* Select the **Create** tab and click **Table** in the Tables group.

To create your table and display it in Design view:

* Select the **Create** tab and click **Table Design** in the **Tables** group.

In Datasheet view, the table is displayed in the right pane, and the table name is displayed in the Navigation Pane on the left. Initially, the table is given the temporary name *Table1*. When you save the table, this should be changed to something that reflects its contents.

The Datasheet tab is displayed, with buttons that perform various tasks that are useful when working in Datasheet view.

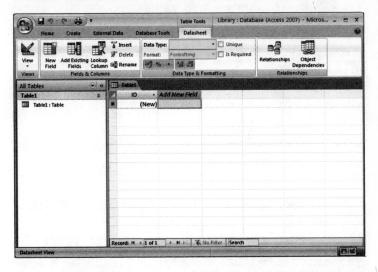

To save your table:

1 Click the **Save** tool on the Quick Access toolbar.

2 Give your table a name in the **Save As** dialog box.

3 Click **OK**.

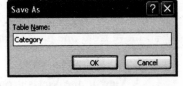

You should always save your table after you have changed its structure – it is not saved automatically. If you try to do anything without first saving the table, Access will prompt you to save it.

To go into Design view:

◆ Click the **View** button in the **Views** group at the left of the **Datasheet** tab.

The Design tab is displayed, with buttons that perform various tasks that are useful when working in Design view. In Design view you can specify the field names, data types and any other properties you think would be useful.

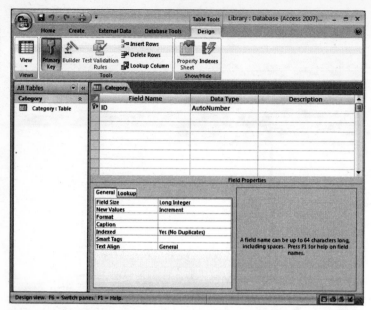

The Design view window has two panes – an upper one where you specify the field name, data type and description, and a lower one where you specify the field properties.

- To move from one pane to the other, press [F6].

To return to Datasheet view:

- Click **View** in the **Views** group on the **Design** tab.

You can also use the **View** tools at the bottom right of the screen to change views.

Datasheet view ——— Design view

Pivot Table   Pivot Chart

Close and open tables

Once you have finished working on your table you can close it.

- To close a table, click the **Close** button. You can close the table from Datasheet or Design view.

- To open a table, double-click on its name in the Navigation pane.

3.2 Data types and properties

Data types

There are eleven different data types to choose from when setting up your table structures. Brief notes on each type are given in the table below for your information. Most of your fields will probably be **Text**, with a few of the others used in each table depending on the type of data you wish to store.

Data Type	Usage	Size	Notes
Text	Alphanumeric data	up to 255 bytes	Default data type
Memo	Alphanumeric data	up to 64 Kbytes	
Number	Numeric data	1, 2, 4 or 8 bytes	Can be used in calculations
Date/Time	Dates and times	8 bytes	Values for the years 100 through to 9999
Currency	Monetary data	8 bytes	Accurate to 4 decimal places and 15 digits to the left of the decimal separator
AutoNumber	Unique long integer created by Access for each new record	4 bytes	Cannot be updated. Useful for primary key fields
Yes/No	Boolean data	1 bit	Yes and No values, and fields that contain 1 of 2 values On/Off, True/False
OLE Object	Pictures, graphs or data objects from other Windows applications	Up to 1 gigabyte	Cannot be indexed
Hyperlink	Inserts a 'hot spot' that lets you jump to another location on your computer, on your intranet or on the Internet	The address can contain up to 3 parts (each part can be up to 2048 characters)	The 3 parts are: Text to display* Address Subaddress* Screentip* * optional
Attachment	Any supported type of file		Images, spreadsheets, documents, charts, etc.
Lookup Wizard	Lets you look up values in another table or from a list	The same as the primary key used to perform the look up	Choosing this option starts the Lookup Wizard to define the data type

Properties

You can customize each field by specifying different properties, which vary depending on the data type. The key properties are:

Property	Data Type	Notes
Field size	Text and Number	Text from 1 to 255 characters
	Number field sizes are: • Byte (single byte) • Integer (2-byte) • Long Integer (4-byte) • Single (4-byte) • Double (8-byte)	Values: • –0 to 255 • –32,768 to +32,767 • –2,147,483,648 to 2,147,483,648 • -3.4×10^{38} to 3.4×10^{38} • -1.797×10^{308} to $+1.797 \times 10^{308}$
Format		Options depend on the data type
Decimal places	Number and Currency	Auto (displays 2 d.p. for most formats except General Number, where decimal places depend on the precision of the number) or Fixed from 0 to 15 d.p.
Input mask	Text, Number, Currency and Date/Time	Uses special characters to show the type of input allowed, and whether or not input is required. See notes on input masks below
Caption		For display on forms and reports
Default value	All data types except Memo, OLE Object and AutoNumber	
Validation rule		You specify conditions to check that only the right sort of data is entered
Validation text		You can specify the message to appear on the screen when a validation rule is not met
Required		Set to Yes if data must be entered
Allow zero length	Text, Memo and Hyperlink fields	
Indexed	Text, Number, Currency, Date/Time and AutoNumber types	Indexing speeds up access to its data – fields that will be sorted or queried on should be indexed. You can insist that data is unique, e.g. ref numbers, or allow duplicates, e.g. names.
Unicode Compression	Text, Memo and Hyperlink fields	Worldwide character encoding standard. Leave at default – *Yes*
SmartTags	Not Y/N, OLE, attachment	Allows SmartTag to be applied to field.

0	Digit (0–9), entry required. Plus (+) and Minus (–) signs not allowed
9	Digit or space. Plus (+) and Minus (–) signs not allowed
#	Digit or space, Plus (+) and Minus (–) signs allowed
L	Letter (A–Z), entry required
?	Letter (A–Z)
A	Letter or digit, entry required
a	Letter or digit
&	Any character or space, entry required
C	Any character or space
<	Convert following characters to lower case
>	Convert following characters to upper case
!	Causes input mask to fill from right to left when characters on the left side of the input mask are optional
\	Causes the following character to be displayed as a literal character, i.e. \L is displayed as L. Entry required.
. , : ; - /	Decimal placeholder and thousand, date and time separators
"Literal text"	Encloses in double quotes any text that you want users to see
Password	Creates a password entry field (must be specified in Design view). When users type in this field, Access stores the characters but displays asterisks (*).

Additional notes

- An input mask can contain up to three sections, separated by a semi-colon, e.g.

    99/99/00;0;_

- The first part specifies the pattern for the mask itself.

- The second part specifies whether or not any literal display characters are stored with the data. The default value is 0 meaning that the characters are stored; 1 means that only the data is stored.

- The final part sets the character used to display spaces in the input mask at data entry. The default is the underline character. If you want to use a space, enclose it in quotes, i.e.

    99/99/00;0;" "

3.3 Setting up a table in Datasheet view

The simplest way to set up your table is in Datasheet view. There are a limited range of commands available on the Datasheet tab that allow you to specify some of the field properties, e.g. data type, format, unique (for primary key fields), required (to specify that a field must have something in it) and number formats, e.g. currency, percentage, comma and increase/decrease decimal places.

Let's say our book categories were:

Adult Fiction	Animals	Astronomy
Children's Fiction	Computing	Cooking
Craft	Education	Family
Foreign Language	Gardening	Geography
Health	History	Music
Poetry	Religion	Romantic Fiction
Science	Travel	

To set up a field for this data:

1 Double-click in the column heading 2 – where it says **Add New Field**.

2 Type in your field name – *Category*.

3 Click in the first row of the Datasheet.

4 Type in your first entry.

5 Press [**Tab**] to move through the fields, entering the data as you go.

6 Save the table – call it *Category*.

7 Close the table.

Things to note:

• The ID field increments automatically. This is because its data type is set to AutoNumber.

• Access determines the data type of the *Category* field based on the data entered – it is set to Text as the entries are text.

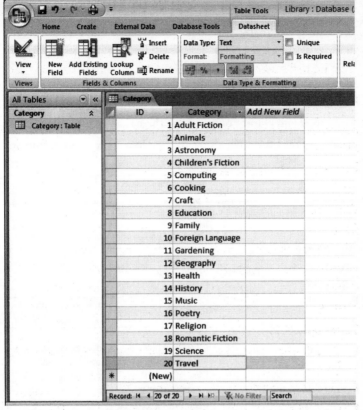

Navigation buttons

- The Data Type & Formatting tools on the Datasheet tab contain the most regularly-used field properties. The options that are available depend on the data type of the field you are in.

- The navigation buttons at the bottom of the window help you move through your records. The current record number and the total number of records is also displayed here.

- The column widths can be adjusted by dragging the vertical bar to the right of the field name.

- Once a table has been saved, the data that you enter and edit is automatically saved as you work.

3.4 Setting up a table in Design view

Try setting up the book table in Design view. The data types and field properties for each field are suggested below. Create a new table in Design view (see section 3.1).

Setting up the ISBN field

1 In the **Field Name** column, type the name – *ISBN* in our case.

2 Press [**Tab**] to move along to the **Data Type** column and set this to **Text**.

Book Table			
Field Name	**Data Type**	**Properties**	**Notes**
ISBN	Text	Field Size = 20 Required = Yes	Primary key
Title	Text	Field Size = 50	
AuthorID	Number	Long Integer	
PublisherID	Number	Long Integer	
Category Name	Text	Field Size = 25	Value will be 'looked up' in the Category table
Row Number	Number	Integer Validation Rule >=1 and <=40 Validation Text 'Enter a number between 1 and 40'	Rows numbered 1–40 if an incorrect entry is made, display the validation text message
Shelf Number	Number	Integer Validation Rule >=1 and <=6 Validation Text 'Enter a number between 1 and 6'	Shelves numbered 1–6, if an incorrect entry is made, display the validation text message
Number of copies	Number	Integer	
Publication Year	Number	Integer	Year only – use Number data type
Price	Currency		
Reference	Yes/No		
Lending	Yes/No	Default value = Yes	
Picture	OLE object		Illustration for book
Additional information	Attachment		Background information & summary of book

3 Press [Tab] to move along to the **Description** column and enter a field description if you wish.

Field properties

1 Press [**F6**] to move to the lower pane (or click with the mouse) and change the field size from 255 to 20.

2 Set the **Required** property to *Yes* – a book must have an ISBN.

3 Press [**F6**] to return to the upper pane.

Establishing the primary key status

The *ISBN* field is the primary key for this table.

◆ Click the **Primary Key** button in the Tools group when the insertion point is anywhere in the *ISBN* field row in the upper pane.

Primary Key

Complete the structure for the rest of the table following the guidelines in the previous table. See notes below regarding the *CategoryName* field specification. Any field that you think you will want to sort on or query should be indexed. This enables Access to sort or select on that field faster than it would be able to do on a non-indexed field.

CategoryName Field

1 Select **Lookup Wizard...** from the **Data Type** list. This invokes the wizard to walk you through the setup process.

2 At the first dialog box, choose '**I want the lookup column to look up the values in another table or query**' and click **Next** (you want to look up the values in the *Category* table).

3 Select the *Category* table from the list and click **Next**.

4 Move the *Category* field from the **Available Fields:** list to the **Selected Fields:** list (select the *Category* field in the **Available Fields:** list and click the top button between the two lists to move it over) and click **Next**.

5 Sort the field in **Ascending** order, click **Next**.

6 Adjust the width of the column if necessary (instructions are on the screen) and click **Next**.

7 Check the suggested column label, and change it if you wish – I suggest you change it to *Category*, as that is the data that will be displayed in the column.

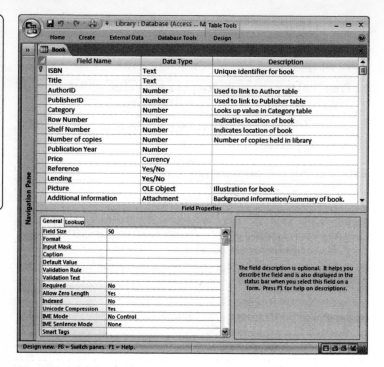

8 Click **Finish**.

9 You will be prompted to save the table on completion of the Wizard. I suggest that you choose '*Yes*' (even if you have not set up the whole table structure yet) and name it *Book*.

The completed structure should be similar to the previous picture.

Save the table design

♦ When you have finished setting up the whole table, remember to Save 🖫 the *Book* table and **Close** ✕ the **Table Design** window.

If you have already saved an earlier version of the table, clicking the Save tool will replace the old version of the table on your disk with the new one.

3.5 Defining the Author table

The Author table is set up in a similar way. Set up the table in Design view, following the guidelines below.

Author Table			
Field Name	**Data Type**	**Properties**	**Notes**
AuthorID	AutoNumber	Long Integer	Primary Key
Surname	Text	Size = 20 Indexed = Yes Duplicates OK	
Firstname	Text	Size = 20 Indexed = Yes Duplicates OK	
Date of Birth	Date/Time	Pick a Format Input mask = 99/99/0000	Type in the code, or click the Build button beside the Input Mask field and work through the Wizard
Date of Death	Date/Time	Pick a Format Input mask = 99/99/0000	Type in the code, or click the Build button beside the Input Mask field and work through the Wizard
Nationality	Text	Size = 25 Indexed = Yes Duplicates OK	
Speciality	Text	Size = 20 Indexed = Yes Duplicates OK	Enter description: 'Main area of author's work'
Notes		Memo	

* Save ▣ the table – call it *Author* – and close ▨ the **Table Design** window.

3.6 Table templates

The last table structure to be set up is the *Publisher* table. This is essentially just a name and address table which could be set up manually, just as we have set up the other three tables. We could also consider using a template to help automate the setting up of this one. Templates can save you time when it comes to setting up a table structure – there are several provided with often-used structures for different situations, including name and address structures.

1 Display the **Create** tab in the Ribbon.

2 Click **Table Templates** and choose **Contacts** from the list.

◆ A new table is created, and it is displayed in Datasheet view.

3 Save the table – call it *Publisher* – and take the table into Design view.

Adjust the field structure and properties to this:

Publisher Table		
Field name	**Data type**	**Properties**
PublisherID	AutoNumber	Primary key
Company	Text	Size = 50
Address 1	Text	Size = 25
Address 2	Text	Size = 25
City	Text	Size = 30
Postcode	Text	Size = 14
County	Text	Size = 30
Country	Text	Size = 20
Phone Number	Text	Size = 30
Fax Number	Text	Size = 30
E-mail address	Text	Size = 40
Website	Hyperlink	

To delete a field:

1 Click anywhere in the field.

2 Click ⇒ **Delete Rows** in the Tools group.

To move a field:

1 In the upper pane, click in the row selector bar to the left of the field you wish to move.

2 With the pointer over the selector bar area, drag and drop the field into its new position – you will notice a thick dark horizontal line that shows where the field will move to.

◆ Save and close the *Publisher* table.

We will look again at editing the table structure in Chapter 5.

Selector bar

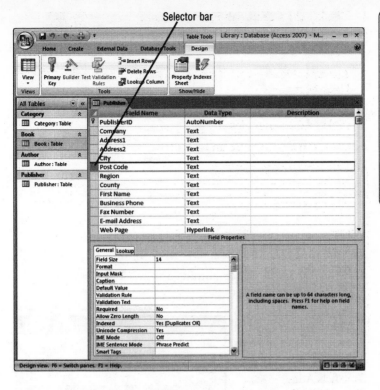

3.7 Relationships

Once the table structures have been set up, you should establish
the relationships between your tables.

To display the relationships tab:

1 Select the **Database Tools** on the
Ribbon.

2 Click **Relationships** in the **Show/
Hide** group.

The Relationships tab will be displayed, with the Category and
Book tables related through the Category field (this is the result
of the lookup field created earlier).

The key icon to their left identifies the primary key fields.

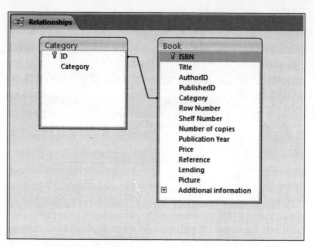

To add more tables to the tab:

1 Click the **Show Table** button in the **Relationships** group.

2 Select the table(s) that you want to add to the **Relationships** tab.

3 Click **Add**.

4 Close the dialog box once all tables have been added.

To add several tables at once:

1 If the tables are listed next to each other in the **Show Table** dialog box, select the first, then point to the last, hold down [**Shift**] and click – all the tables in the range will be selected.

• If the tables are not next to each other, click on the first, then hold down [**Ctrl**] while you click on each of the other tables.

2 Click **Close** once you have added your tables.

Your **Relationships** window will contain all the tables and any relationships will be displayed.

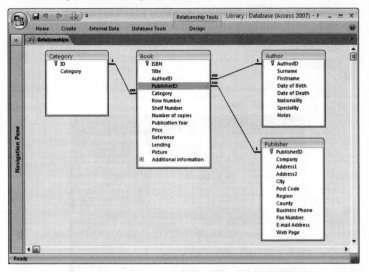

The lines running between the fields linking the tables are called **join lines**. Access will often create the link between tables automatically, e.g. when you use the Lookup Wizard or create tables using the wizard.

* To remove a table from the Relationship window, click on it, then press [**Delete**].

Deleting and creating join lines

You can delete and create other join lines as required.

To delete an existing relationship:

1 Click on the join line you wish to remove.

2 Press [**Delete**].

3 Respond to the prompt as required.

To create a relationship:

1 Click on the field you wish to relate to another table.

2 Drag the selected field and drop it onto the field you wish to link it to in the other table.

3 If you want to check the type of relationship that will be created, click **Join Type...** to view the options in the **Join Properties** dialog box.

4 Change the type if necessary – all our join types should be option 1.

5 Click **OK**.

6 At the **Edit Relationships** dialog box, click **Create** to establish the relationship.

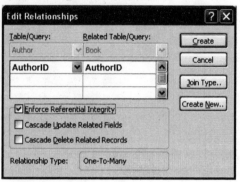

Editing relationships

You can easily edit existing relationships.

1 Double-click the join line that you wish to edit.

2 Modify the settings in the **Edit Relationships** dialog box as necessary.

3 Click **OK**.

Relationship type

One-to-many – one of the related fields is a primary key or contains a unique index. This is the most common type of relationship. In our example a record in the *Publisher* table can have many matching records in *Book*, but a record in the *Book* table has only one matching record in *Publisher* – a one-to-many relationship.

One-to-one – both the related fields are primary keys or contain unique indexes. Each record in the first table can have only one matching record in the second, and vice versa. One-to-one relationships are sometimes used to divide a table that has many fields, or to isolate some fields for security reasons. This type of relationship is not very common.

Indeterminate – neither of the related fields are primary keys or contain unique indexes.

Referential integrity

These are the rules that are followed to preserve the defined relationships between tables when you enter or delete records.

If you enforce referential integrity, Access prevents you from:

- Adding records to a related table when there is no associated record in the primary table.

- Changing values in the primary table that would result in orphan (unconnected) records in a related table.

- Deleting records from the primary table when there are matching related records in a related table.

Save and closing the Relationships tab

1 Click **Save** on the Quick Access toolbar.

2 Click **Close** in the **Relationships** group.

If you close the Relationships tab without saving your changes, you will be prompted to do so. Respond as necessary.

Summary

In this chapter we have discussed the alternative ways of creating the tables within your database:

- Creating a table in Datasheet view

- Creating a table in Design view

- Data types available

- Data properties

- Creating a table using a template

- Checking, creating and deleting relationships between tables.

04

data entry and edit

In this chapter you will learn:

- how to enter and edit data in the datasheet
- some formatting options for the datasheet
- how to move between the different table views

4.1 Data entry in Datasheet view

If you are working through the project in this book, you should be in Access with your *Library* database open. The four tables that we defined in Chapter 3 will be listed under **Tables** in the Navigation pane.

We have already entered our data into the *Category* table.

I suggest you complete the *Publisher* and *Author* tables before the *Book* table – this way you will have the necessary codes for the PublisherID and Author ID fields in the Book table.

Data entry is mostly very easy. You simple open the table and key in the data – using [Tab] or the mouse to move from field to field. As you are keying in the data, look out for the features mentioned below.

• To open a table in **Datasheet** view, double-click on its name, in the Navigation pane.

In Datasheet view, a table looks similar to a spreadsheet layout – each record is presented in a row and each field in a column.

• To move forward through the fields press **[Tab]**.
• To move backwards through the fields press **[Shift]-[Tab]**.
• Or click in the field you want to move to using the mouse.

Project data

If you are working through the library project in this book, key in the data suggested for all four tables. You will find suggested data for each of the tables in the Appendix.

Publisher table
AutoNumber

The *PublisherID* field has the AutoNumber data type – this field will be completed automatically by Access; you cannot enter any data into it.

• Press **[Tab]** to move from column to column, entering your publisher data.

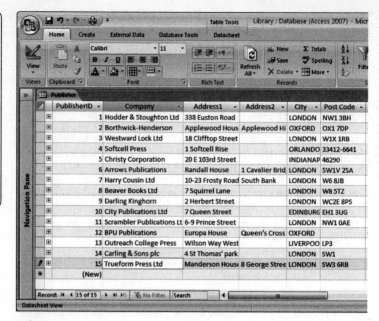

When you complete a record (when you reach the last column):

• Press **[Tab]** to move on to the first column of the next record.

You may notice, as you key in your data, that the record you are currently writing to has a pencil icon in the row selector area to the left of the record.

Hyperlink

You can type the URL directly into the *Website* field if you wish. However, you may prefer a more user-friendly display for the text in the field. The text displayed can really be anything – and you can set the actual URL behind the scenes.

To set up your hyperlink field:

• Type the URL into the field.

Or

1 Right-click in the Hyperlink field.

2 Choose **Hyperlink**, then **Edit Hyperlink...** from the context menu.

3 Select *Existing File or Web Page* in the **Link to:** options.

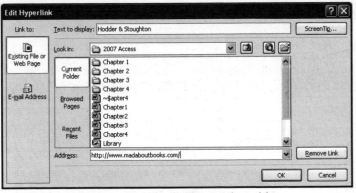

4 Enter the text you wish to display in the table.

5 Type in the URL of the page you want to jump to.

6 Click **OK** at the **Edit Hyperlink** dialog box – your hyperlink text will be displayed, e.g. 'Hodder & Stoughton'.

To jump to a hyperlink location from your table:

♦ Click on the hyperlink.

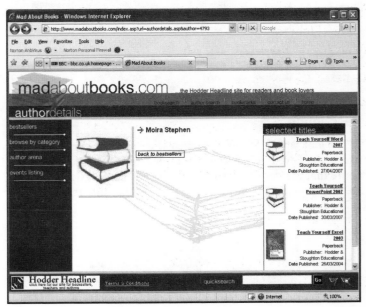

Author table
Input mask

When entering data to the *Author* table, note the effect of the input mask on the *Date of Birth* and *Date of Death* fields. When you enter data into these fields, the pattern set for the data appears and you just key in the figures.

Access also carries out its own validation tests on data that you key into a date field. If you try entering a date like 30/02/60 you will get an error message to indicate the date is not recognized.

	AuthorID	Surname	Firstname	Date of Birth	Date of Death	Nationality
⊞	3	Jackson	Marion	24/06/1955		English
⊞	4	Adamson	Pauline			Australian
⊞	5	Duncan	Wilma	04/07/1938		American
⊞	6	Ferguson	John	03/04/1903	05/10/1988	Irish
⊞	7	Jackson	Allan	10/12/1940	02/10/1993	Scottish
⊞	8	Smith	Dick			Canadian
⊞	9	Schmit	Hans	12/12/1952		German
⊞	10	Camembert	Marion			French
⊞	11	Meunier	Luc			French
⊞	12	Allan	Isabelle	10/04/1965		Scottish
⊞	13	Stephen	Moira			Scottish
⊞	14	MacDonald	Donald	12/12/1920	01/03/1978	Scottish
⊞	15	Williams	Peter	10/10/1930		Irish
⊞	16	Borthwick	Anne			Welsh
⊞	17	Ferguson	Alan	04/12/1945	/ /	English
⊞	18	Wilson	Peter	12/01/1930		Canadian
⊞	19	Smith	Ann			American

Description

If you look at the Status bar when entering data into a field for which you keyed in a description during table definition, you will notice that the description text appears in the status bar when you are in that field, e.g. the *Speciality* field for the *Author* table.

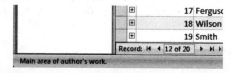

⊞	17	Ferguso
⊞	18	Wilson
⊞	19	Smith

Record: ◄ ◄ 12 of 20 ► ►► ►

Main area of author's work.

Book table

Category field

When the insertion point is in the *Category* field:

1 Click the drop-down arrow on the right.

2 Select the name required from the list (the entries in the list have been looked up in the *Category* table).

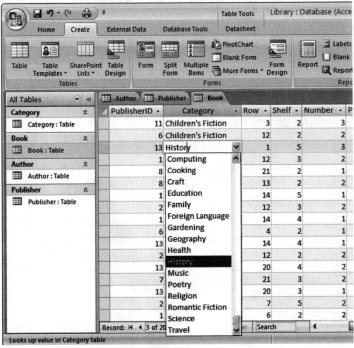

Validation rules and validation text

Check out your validation codes in the *Row Number* and *Shelf Number* fields by entering a shelf number over 40 and a row number over 6.

Yes/No fields

In the *Book* table we defined the **Yes/No** data type for the *Reference* and *Lending* fields. On entering data in Datasheet view notice that they are displayed as checkboxes.

- To register a 'Yes' there must be a tick in the box.
- To register a 'No' leave the box empty.

You can toggle the status of this field by clicking on the box.

Default Value

Notice that the *Lending* field has been selected automatically for each record. This is because we set the Default Value to **Yes** when we defined the table.

OLE Object

In the Book table we defined an OLE Object data type for the Picture field to allow us to insert a picture that reflected the book's subject. An easy way to insert a picture is to drag and drop it from the Clip Organizer into the OLE object field.

To insert a picture using Drag and Drop:

1 Display the OLE Object field in Datasheet view.

2 Open the Clip Organizer – **Start > All Programs > Microsoft Office > Microsoft Office Tools > Microsoft Clip Organizer.**

3 Browse through the folders until you locate a suitable clip.

4 Resize or reposition the Clip Organizer window as necessary, so that you can see your OLE Object field in Access.

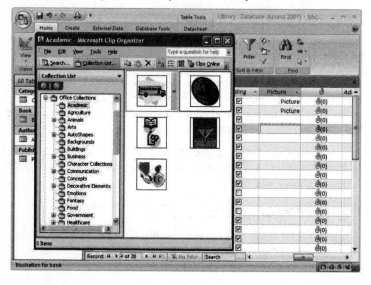

5 Drag and Drop the picture into the field.

♦ In Datasheet view, the object *source* will be identified. i.e. Picture.

♦ In Form view, the object will be displayed.

You can insert other objects into an OLE Object field from the Object... dialog box, which you can open from the Insert menu. Search for "insert object" in the Help system to find out more.

4.2 Datasheet and Design view

If you discover a problem with your table design, you can move from Datasheet view to Design view to fix it.

♦ To move from Datasheet view to Design view, click the **View** button on the **Datasheet** tab.

If you make any changes to the design of your table, you must save them. Be careful not to make any changes that will result in losing data that you need, e.g. making a field too small.

♦ To move back into Datasheet view, click the **View** tool on the **Design** tab.

4.3 Editing in Datasheet view

Moving through your table

We have already discussed the fact that you can move within and between records using the [Tab], [Shift]-[Tab] keyboard techniques, or by pointing and clicking in the desired field using the mouse.

The navigation buttons are displayed at the bottom left of the datasheet. These can be used to help you move through your table in Datasheet view.

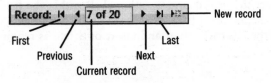

- The record number field tells you which record the insertion point is currently in, and to the right of this you will find the total number of records in your table.

- The **Next** and **Previous Record** buttons allow you to move forwards and backwards through your records, one at a time.

- The current field remains constant as you move up or down through your records – although you are moving from one record to another, the same field in each record is selected.

- The **Last** and **First Record** buttons move you through to the last or first record respectively.

- To go to a specific record, type its number in the record number field and press [**Enter**].

Editing the field contents

If you spot an error in Datasheet view, you must position the insertion point within the field you wish to edit, and make whatever changes are required.

You can use the scroll bars (horizontal and vertical), or the navigation buttons to locate the record you need to update. Once the record has been located, the simplest technique is to click within the field that needs to be changed and insert or delete data as necessary.

If you use the [**Tab**] or [**Shift**]-[**Tab**] keyboard techniques to move through fields that contain data, the contents of a field are selected when you move on to it.

- To replace the selected data within a field, simply key in the new text – whatever you type will replace the original data.

- To delete the data in the field press [**Delete**] when the old data is still selected.

- To add or delete data **without** removing the current contents of the field, you must deselect the field contents before you edit.

To deselect the field contents, either click within the field using your mouse, or press [**F2**]. Once the data is deselected you can position the insertion point and insert or delete as required.

Adding new records

Regardless of which record your insertion point is currently in, the **New Record** button beside the navigation buttons, or the ⊞ New button in the **Records** group on the **Home** tab, takes you to the first empty row at the end of your table, to allow you to add a new record.

4.4 Formatting in Datasheet view

When working in Datasheet view, there are a number of formatting options you might like to experiment with.

Formatting the datasheet affects the whole table, not just the row or column the insertion point is in.

The commands in the Font group are used for most formatting options.

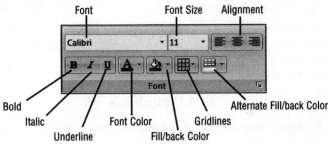

Font   Font Size   Alignment

Bold
Italic   Font Color   Gridlines   Alternate Fill/back Color
Underline   Fill/back Color

To change the font:

1 Click the arrow to the right of the Font button.
2 Scroll through the list of fonts until you see the font you want to use.
3 Click on it.

To change the font size:

1 Click the arrow to the right of the Font Size button.
2 Scroll through the list of sizes until you see the one you want to use.
3 Click on it.

To set bold, italic, underline:

- These formatting options are toggles – click the button to switch them on and off again.

To change the font colour:

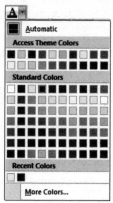

1 Click the arrow to the right of the **Font Color** button.

2 Select the colour you want to use.

Or

- Click **More Colors...** for the full range of colour choices.

Alignment

The alignment of the contents of a field can be left, right or centre. The default alignment is left for text, and right for number, AutoNumber, currency and date fields.

To specify the alignment:

- To left align: click the **Align Left** button ▤.

- To centre align: click the **Centre** button ▤.

- To right align: click the **Align Right** button ▤.

The alignment chosen affects the whole column, not just the field that is selected.

Fill/back colour

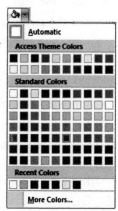

Selecting a fill/back colour has the effect of adding colour to alternate rows in your table, often making it easier to read. The command affects the odd record numbers, i.e. 1, 3, 5, 7, etc.

1 Click the **Fill/back color** button in the Font group.

2 Pick a colour, or click **More Colors...** to get additional colours and shades to choose from.

Gridlines

By default, both horizontal and vertical gridlines are displayed in your datasheet. You can control this using the **Gridlines** button if you wish.

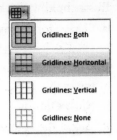

Alternate Fill/back colour

This option works with the Fill/back colour command. The colour chosen will affect your even records, i.e. 2, 4, 6, 8, etc.

More options

If you click the dialog box launcher in the Font group it will display the Datasheet Formatting dialog box where you can add special effects, e.g. sunken, raised to your datasheet, choose alternate gridline colours, and customize the border and line styles.

Other formatting options are changing the row height and/or the column width.

To change the row height:

1 Position the mouse pointer over the dark line between two rows – you should get a black double-headed pointer.

2 Click and drag up or down until the required height is reached.

To set the row height to a specific value:

1 Click **More** in the **Records** group.

2 Choose **Row Height...**

3 Specify the height (in points) in the dialog box.

4 Click **OK**.

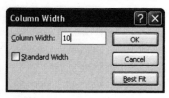

To change the column width:

1 Position the pointer over the dark line to the right of the field name of the column – you should get a black double-headed pointer.

2 Click and drag right or left to make the column to the left bigger or smaller.

To set the column width to a specific value:

1 Click **More** in the **Records** group.

2 Choose **Column Width...**

3 Specify the width (in characters) in the dialog box and click **OK**.

Or

♦ Click **Best Fit** to get Access to work out the column width based on the data in the field.

4.5   Data entry in Form view

As an alternative to entering data into a table in Datasheet view, you could use a form.

In Datasheet view, each record is displayed in a row, each field in a column. As many fields and records are displayed in the table window as will fit. In a form, the fields are arranged on the screen (you can design forms to resemble the paper forms you actually use) and one record is displayed at a time. A form is often considered more user-friendly than Datasheet view.

To create a basic form:

1 In the Navigation pane, select the table for which to create a form.

- Open the table in Datasheet view.

2 Click **Form** in the **Forms** group on the **Create** tab.

If the form is at the **many** side of a relationship, it will be display the first record in that table. You can move through the records using the Navigation buttons, just as you would in the table.

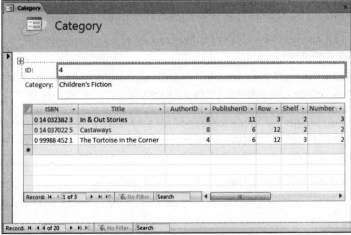

If the form is based on a table at the **one** side of a one-to-many relationship, the table from the one side of the relationship is displayed at the top of the form, and the related records from the table at the many side are displayed below this.

ISBN	Title	AuthorID	PublisherID	Row	Shelf	Number
0 14 032382 3	In & Out Stories	8	11	3	2	3
0 14 037022 5	Castaways	8	6	12	2	2
0 99988 452 1	The Tortoise in the Corner	4	6	12	3	2

Notice the two sets of Navigation buttons. The upper ones in this example belong to the *Book* table (at the many side of the relationship), and the lower ones belong to the *Category* table (at the one side of the relationship).

You can move around a form in the same way as you did your Datasheet.

* Press [Tab] or [Shift]-[Tab] to move from field to field, or click in the field you want to input or edit.

* Use the navigation buttons to move from record to record, or to the first or last record in the table.

* To go to a specific record, type the number in the record number field, and press [**Enter**].

* Click the **New Record** button to get a blank form on which to enter new data.

* If necessary, use the scroll bars to display parts of the form that are not displayed in the window.

The data you enter or edit in your form in Form view will be stored in the table on which the form is based. Even if you opt not to save the form itself, the data will still be stored.

Any fields defined as an OLE Object (e.g. the *Picture* field in the *Book* table) will display the object in Form view, but the name of the source application is shown in Datasheet view.

View options

When working with a Form you have three view options to choose from – Layout, Form or Design.

Layout view

The forms are displayed in Layout view when you create them in this way. In Layout view, you can edit the structure of the form to a limited extent. The data from the underlying table is displayed in the fields (controls) on your form. We will discuss form layout in Chapter 6.

Form view

You can enter and edit your data in Form view.

- To go into Form view, click the **View** button in the **Views** group of the **Home** tab.

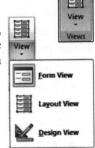

- To return to Layout view, click the **View** button again.

If you click the arrow below the **View** button, all the view options that are currently available are displayed. For the time being, stick with Layout and Form views.

- Once a form has been created, saved and closed, it will open in Form view the next time you open it.

We will look at editing the form layout and working in Design view in Chapter 6.

Saving your form

If you want to save your form:

1 Click the **Save** tool on the Quick Access toolbar.

2 At the **Save As** dialog box, either accept the default form name, or edit it as required.

3 Click **OK**.

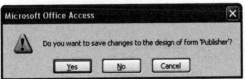

If you close your form without first saving it, Access will ask you if you want to save the form.

If you choose **Yes**, you will be taken to the **Save As** dialog box. If you choose **No**, the form will close without being saved. If you click **Cancel**, you will be returned to the form.

If you save your form, it will be listed in the Navigation pane. You can open the form again at any time – either double-click on the form name or select it and click **Open**.

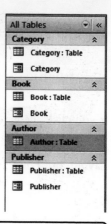

Summary

In this chapter we have considered the main options for entering and editing data in your tables. You have found out about:

- Opening your tables in Datasheet view

- Entering and editing data in Datasheet view

- Moving between records

- Adding new records

- Formatting the datasheet

- Moving between the different table view options

- Creating a simple form

- Entering data in Form view

- Saving a form.

05

table manipulation

In this chapter you will learn:

- how to edit a table structure
- how to add and delete records
- about hiding and freezing columns
- how to preview and print your table

5.1 Changing the table structure

The table structure can be adjusted in Datasheet or in Design view. There are a limited number of field property options in Datasheet view – the complete range is available in Design view.

Datasheet view

Field properties

To change the properties of a field in Datasheet view, use the buttons in the **Data Type & Formatting** group.

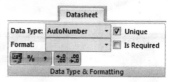

* **Data Type:** Click the drop-down arrow to display a list where you can select an alternative data type.

* **Format:** The options in this list vary, depending on the data type selected.

* **Currency, Percent** and **Comma** are formatting options that can be used on Number fields.

* **Increase Decimal** and **Decrease Decimal** are used to control the accuracy of the figures displayed.

* The **Unique** checkbox determines whether or not duplicate values are allowed. A Primary Key field would be unique.

* **Is Required** determines whether or not a field must contain data.

Rename a field

To change the field name from Datasheet view:

1 Double-click in the field name at the top of the column.

2 Edit the field as required and press **[Enter]**.

Or

1 Click anywhere within the field.

2 Click **Rename** in the **Fields & Columns** group on the **Datasheet** tab.

3 Edit the field and press **[Enter]**.

To delete a field in Datasheet view:

1 Click anywhere within the field.

2 Click **Delete** in the **Fields & Columns** group.

Or

1 Select the column.

2 Click **Delete** in the **Records** group on the **Home** tab.

Or

1 Click anywhere within the field (column).

2 Click the arrow to the right of **Delete** in the **Records** group.

3 Choose **Delete Column**.

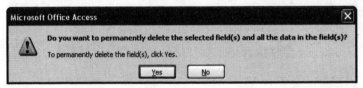

You will be prompted if you choose to delete. Click **Yes** if you are sure, and **No** if you don't really want to delete the field.

Take care with this – don't delete a field if you don't really want to!! You can't undo to restore it – you'll have to type it back in!

To add a new field:

1 Click anywhere within the field that will go to the right of your new field.

2 Click **Insert** in the **Fields & Columns** group.

3 Enter your data.

To add a new field at the end of your datasheet:

◆ Click **New Field** in the **Fields & Columns** group.

Or

1 Double-click on **Add New Field** at the top of the next empty column.

2 Enter the field name.

3 Click in the row below the field name.

4 Enter your data.

- If you press [Tab] or [Enter] once you have added the field name, you will move to the column heading at the top of the next field – so you can add several fields one after the other.

To move a field:

1 Select the column – click at the top of it.
2 Point at the field name with the mouse pointer.
3 Drag and drop the field in the required position.
4 Save the changes.

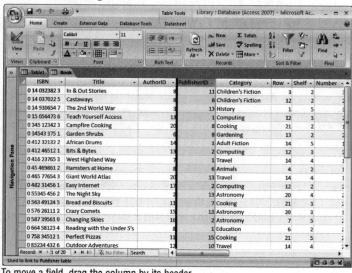

To move a field, drag the column by its header.

Design view

To change a field name:

- Edit the field name in the upper pane.

To change the data type:

- Select an alternative data type in the upper pane.

To adjust a field's properties:

1 Click within the field in the upper pane.
2 Press [F6] (or click) – in the lower pane.
3 Adjust the properties as necessary.

To delete a field:

1 Click within the field row in the upper pane.

2 Click **Delete Rows** in the **Tools** group. | ⇛ Delete Rows

3 Respond to the prompt as necessary.

To add a new field:

If the field has to go at the end of the table structure, click in the first empty row and enter the table name, data type, etc.

If the field has to go between other fields:

1 Click anywhere in the row below where you want the new field positioned.

2 Click **Insert Rows** in the **Tools** group. | ╕¤ Insert Rows

3 Add the field details and properties.

To move a field:

1 Select the row – click the selector area to the left of the name.

2 Point to the row selector box with the mouse pointer.

3 Drag and Drop the field in the required position.

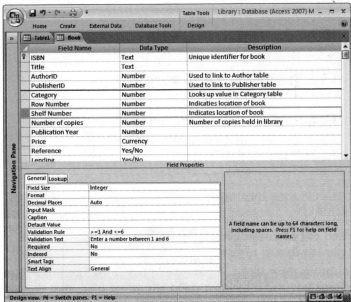

Moving a field in Design view.

Primary key

To change the field that has primary key status:

◆ In the upper pane, place the insertion point in the field that you want to take primary key status. Click the **Primary Key** tool.

To remove primary key status, and not give it to any other field:

◆ In the upper pane, click into the field that has primary key status and click the **Primary Key** tool.

5.2 Adding and deleting records

When adding new records you add them to the end of the list of existing records.

To add a new record:

1 Click the **New Record** button in the **Records** group on the **Home** tab to move through to the first empty row under the existing records.

2 Key in your data.

To delete a record in Datasheet view:

1 Select the row.

2 Click **Delete** in the **Records** group.

Or

1 Click anywhere within the record (row).

2 Click the arrow to the right of **Delete** in the **Records** group.

3 Choose **Delete Record**.

You will be prompted if you choose to delete the record. Clicking **Yes** if you are sure, and **No** if you don't really want to.

5.3 Subdatasheet

A subdatasheet is simply a datasheet that is located within another datasheet. The subdatasheet will contain records that are related or joined to records in the first datasheet.

Access automatically creates a subdatasheet in a table that is in a one-to-one relationship, or is on the one side of a one-to-many relationship, when the Subdatasheet Name property of the table is set to *Auto*. (You can check this setting from Design view for any table – click **Property Sheet** on the Table Design toolbar.) A relationship is defined by matching primary and foreign key fields in the related tables.

Property Sheet

All of the tables in our database are related to at least one other in the database. The *Publisher*, *Author* and *Category* tables are each related to one table, *Book*, in a one-to-many relationship.

PublisherID	Company	Address1	Address2	City	Post Code	Region	Country	Business P
1	Hodder & Stoughton Ltd	338 Euston Road		LONDON	NW1 3BH		England	0207 738 6

ISBN	Title	AuthorID	Category	Row	Shelf	Number	Publication	Pri
0 15 056473 6	Teach Yourself Access 2003	13	Computing	12	3	2	2003	
0 412 32132 2	African Drums	14	Adult Fiction	14	5	1	1992	
0 416 23765 3	West Highland Way	7	Travel	14	4	1	2002	
0 664 58123 4	Reading with the Under 5's	8	Education	6	2	2	2005	

	PublisherID	Company	Address1	Address2	City	Post Code	Region	Country	Business P
⊞	2	Borthwick-Henderson	Applewood Hous	Applewood Hi	OXFORD	OX1 7DP	Oxfordshir	England	01865 3339
⊞	3	Westward Lock Ltd	18 Clifftop Street		LONDON	W1X 1RB		England	0207 333 4
⊞	4	Softcell Press	1 Softcell rise		ORLANDO	33412-6641	Florida	USA	
⊞	5	Christy Corporation	20 E 103rd Street		INDIANAP	46290		USA	
⊞	6	Arrows Publications	Randall House	1 Cavalier Brid	LONDON	SW1V 2SA		England	0207 443 9
⊞	7	Harry Cousin Ltd	10-23 Frosty Road	South Bank	LONDON	W6 8JB		England	0208 444 0
⊞	8	Beaver Books Ltd	7 Squirrel Lane		LONDON	W8 5TZ		England	0207 445 7
⊞	9	Darling Kinghorn	2 Herbert Street		LONDON	WC2E 8PS		England	0208 665 7
⊞	10	City Publications Ltd	7 Queen Street		EDINBURG	EH1 3UG	Midlothiar	Scotland	0131 445 6
⊞	11	Scrambler Publications Lt	6-9 Prince Street		LONDON	NW1 0AE		England	0208 556 4
⊞	12	BPU Publications	Europa House	Queen's Cross	OXFORD			Oxfordshir	England	
⊞	13	Outreach College Press	Wilson Way West		LIVERPOO	LP3		England	
⊞	14	Carling & Sons plc	4 St Thomas' park		LONDON	SW1		England	
⊞	15	Trueform Press Ltd	Manderson Hous	8 George Stree	LONDON	SW3 6RB		England	0207 334 3
*	(New)								

When looking at a table in Datasheet view, you can tell that it has a subdatasheet attached to it if the first column in the table is filled with ⊞.

To view the related data, click the ⊞ to expand the subdatasheet.

To collapse the subdatasheet again, click ⊟ in the first column.

There may be times when you want to expand (or collapse) the subdatasheets of all records in the table displayed.

To expand (or collapse) the subdatasheets of all the records:

1 Click **More** in the Records group on the **Home** tab.

2 Select **Subdatasheet**.

3 Choose **Expand All** or **Collapse All** as required.

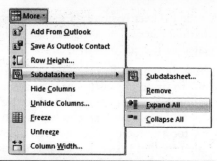

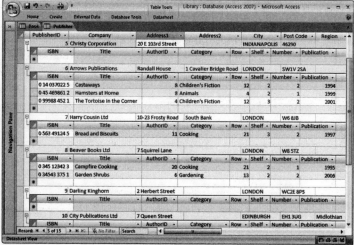

You can enter and edit data in the main table or the subdatasheet as necessary.

To remove a subdatasheet link:

1 Click **More** in the **Records** group on the **Home** tab.

2 Select **Subdatasheet**.

3 Choose **Remove**.

The left-most column in your table will disappear and the link between the tables is gone.

To restore the link again:

1 Click **More** in the **Records** group on the **Home** tab.

2 Select **Subdatasheet** then **Subdatasheet...**

3 In the **Insert Sub-datasheet** dialog box, select the table to link to.

4 Check/edit the fields through which the tables are linked

5 Click **OK**.

5.4 Hiding columns

When working in Datasheet view, the number of fields displayed and the horizontal scroll required to move from the first field to the last field in a record can make it difficult to view the data you require. You may find yourself scrolling back and forward checking and double checking field contents.

If you aren't interested in the contents of some fields for the time being, you can hide the fields you don't need.

When you hide columns, they aren't deleted but simply hidden from view.

To hide fields you must first select them.

To select a single field:

◆ Click inside the column you wish to hide.

To select adjacent columns:

There are two methods to choose from when selecting several adjacent columns:

◆ Click and drag in the **Field Name** row (when the pointer is a solid black arrow) across the columns.

Or

1 Select the first field by clicking anywhere in it.

2 Scroll through the columns until you can see the last column in the group you require.

3 Hold down [Shift] and click in the Field Name row at the top of the last column to be selected. All the fields between the first and last column will be selected.

4 Click More in the Records group on the Home tab.

5 Select Hide Columns.

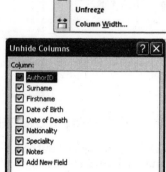

To unhide columns again:

1 Click More in the Records group.

2 Select Unhide Columns...

3 Select the fields you want to display and click Close.

5.5 Freezing columns

When you freeze a column or columns, they become the leftmost columns in your table. Columns that are frozen do not scroll off the screen – they remain static while the other columns in your table scroll in and out of view.

To freeze a column or columns:

1 Select the column(s).

2 Click More in the Records group on the Home tab.

3 Choose Freeze.

If the column(s) you choose are not at the left side of the table, they will be moved there.

If you need to freeze columns that are not adjacent to each other, select and freeze them one by one until you have built up the arrangement of frozen columns required. Once the columns are

Frozen columns

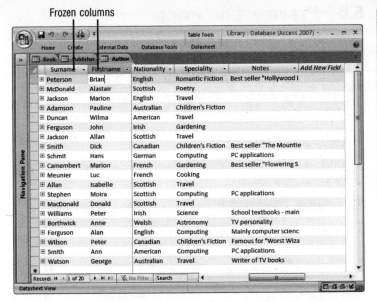

frozen you can scroll the other columns in and out of view as required – the frozen ones will remain at the left. On your screen, you will notice a dark vertical line between the frozen columns and unfrozen columns.

To unfreeze a column or columns:

1 Click **More** in the **Records** group on the **Home** tab.

2 Choose **Unfreeze**.

The columns that are unfrozen remain to the left of the table – you have effectively rearranged the fields and placed those that were frozen at the beginning of the table.

Closing the table

When you close your table, you will be asked if you want to save the changes to the layout of your table.

If you choose **Yes** the new field order will be saved, if you choose **No** the fields will remain in the order they were before you froze them.

5.6 Preview and Print

Print Preview

Before printing your table, it is recommended that you do a print preview to check that it will look okay on the page. You can either select the table on the Navigation panel or display the table in Datasheet view to do this.

To preview your table:

♦ Click the Microsoft Office button, choose **Print**, then **Print Preview**.

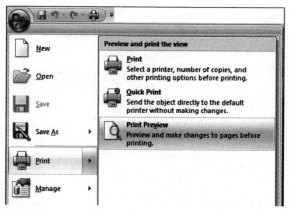

A preview of your datasheet will be displayed.

ISBN	Title	AuthorID	PublisherID	Category	Row Nu	Shelf Nu	Number of c
0 14 032382 3	In & Out Stories	8		11 Children's Fiction	3	2	3
0 14 037022 5	Castaways	8		6 Children's Fiction	12	2	2
0 14 930654 7	The 2nd World War	3		13 History	1	5	3
0 15 056473 6	Teach Yourself Access	13		1 Computing	12	3	2
0 345 12342 3	Campfire Cooking	20		8 Cooking	21	2	1
0 34543 375 1	Garden Shrubs	6		8 Gardening	13	2	2
0 412 32132 2	African Drums	14		1 Adult Fiction	14	5	1
0 412 46512 1	Bits & Bytes	13		2 Computing	12	3	2
0 416 23765 3	West Highland Way	7		1 Travel	14	4	1
0 45 469861 2	Hamsters at Home	8		6 Animals	4	2	1
0 465 77654 3	Giant World Atlas	20		13 Travel	14	4	1
0 482 31456 1	Easy Internet	17		2 Computing	12	2	2
0 55345 456 2	The Night Sky	2		13 Astronomy	20	4	2
0 563 49124 5	Bread and Biscuits	11		7 Cooking	21	3	2
0 576 26111 2	Crazy Comets	15		13 Astronomy	20	3	1
0 587 39561 0	Changing Skies	16		2 Astronomy	7	5	2
0 664 58123 4	Reading with the Under 5's	8		1 Education	6	2	2
0 758 34512 1	Perfect Pizzas	11		15 Cooking	21	5	2
0 85234 432 6	Outdoor Adventures	12		10 Travel	14	4	2
0 99988 452 1	The Tortoise in the Corner	4		6 Children's Fiction	12	3	2

Book   20/02/2007

Page 1

Use the Print Preview tab to work with your table. The commands you are most likely to use are:

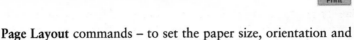

Print – to display the Print dialog box.

Page Layout commands – to set the paper size, orientation and margins for your printout.

An important one in this group is **Page Setup** which displays the **Page Setup** dialog box.

You can set the margins on the **Print Options** tab as well as specifying whether or not you want to print headings, e.g. page number, table name – at the top and bottom of each page.

On the **Page** tab you can set the orientation, page size and printer.

Zoom commands – to display the required number of pages, or Zoom in and out.

Close Preview – which returns you to your database or datasheet view (depending on whether or not the table was open when you previewed it).

Print

You can print your datasheet from Print Preview or from the datasheet itself.

To print your table:

1 Click **Print** on the Ribbon in Print Preview.

To print from the datasheet or the table in the Navigation pane:

* Click the Microsoft Office button, and choose **Print**, then **Print** again.

2 Specify the options required in the **Print** dialog box.

3 Click **OK**.

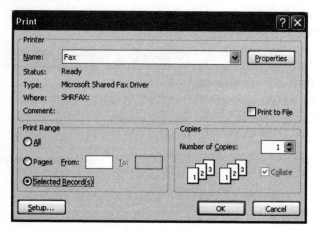

To print selected records:

1 Display your datasheet.

2 Select the records that you want to print – click and drag down the row selector column to the left of the records.

3 Display the **Print** dialog box.

4 Select *Selected Record(s)* in the **Print Range**.

5 Click **OK**.

Summary

In this chapter you have concentrated on a number of techniques that are useful when working with datasheets.

You have learnt how to:

* Change the field properties of existing fields
* Rearrange the fields within your tables
* Rename fields
* Add new records to a table
* Delete records from a table
* Use subdatasheets
* Hide and unhide columns
* Freeze and unfreeze columns
* Preview your table prior to printing
* Print your table.

06

form design

In this chapter you will learn:

- how to design a form
- about some of the objects that you can use on a form
- how to add images to a form
- how to control the tab order
- about printing forms

6.1 Introducing forms

Form tools were introduced in Chapter 4, where we discussed data entry and edit techniques. We used a Form tool to create a basic form layout, showing one record at a time on the form. Forms can be used to display the data from tables or queries (queries will be discussed in Chapter 7). You can use them for entering and editing data.

Controls

The objects on a form are called controls. There are text boxes that display the data held in tables or queries, labels for instructions or headings, image controls for pictures, line and rectangle controls for formatting and design, radio buttons and checkboxes – and many more. We will use some of these in this chapter.

Controls can be bound, unbound, and calculated.

Bound control – the data source is in a table or query.

Unbound control – one that doesn't get its data from a table or a query. They are used to display information or draw lines or rectangles, or add pictures. A label, often used to display a title on a form or report, is an example of an unbound control.

Calculated control – the data is derived from an expression rather than from a table or query. Typically, these expressions perform calculations on your data by adding (or subtracting, multiplying or dividing) the values in fields. An expression can contain a combination of operators (such as = and +), control names, field names, functions and constant values. For example =[Gross Pay]-[Tax] might be used to calculate Net Pay. Or =[Unit Price]*1.25 could be used to increase the unit price by 25%.

We will use the different control types in this chapter.

Views

Form view is where you can enter and edit data freely. The data is stored in the underlying table(s). You cannot change the structure of your form in Form view.

Layout view is new in Access 2007 – it's a bit like a halfway house between Form and Design view. In Layout view, you can change the structure of your form and see the underlying data from your table or query at the same time. Being able to see your data at the same time as you adjust the structure of the form can be useful when deciding on the size that you want a control to be.

You will probably find that you can use Layout view to make most of the design changes you want on your form.

Not all tasks can be performed in Layout view and you may be prompted to switch to Design view to make a particular change.

Design view gives a more detailed view of the form structure. You can't see the underlying data in this view – but there are a much wider range of controls available, e.g. images, lines, rectangles, etc.

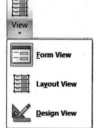

To change from one view to another, use the **View** button on the **Home** tab, or the **View** tools at the bottom right of the window.

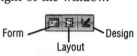

Form — Design
Layout

6.2 Form tools

The Form tools are displayed in the Forms group on the Create tab of the Ribbon. We used the first one, Form, in Chapter 4 (see section 4.5). We will look at some of the others here.

Split Form

The Split Form gives you two views of the same data. The upper part of the form displays one record at a time in a Form layout. The lower part of the form displays several records from the underlying table or query in a layout similar to Datasheet view. The idea is that you can concentrate on one record at time in the upper pane, but keep an eye on the bigger picture of what is happening in the table or query at the same time.

To create a Split Form:

1 Select the table that you want to create a form for in the Navigation panel.

Or

♦ Open the table in Datasheet view.

2 Click **Split Form** in the **Forms** group on the **Create** tab.

You can enter and edit records in either pane.

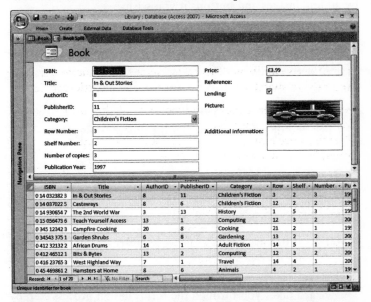

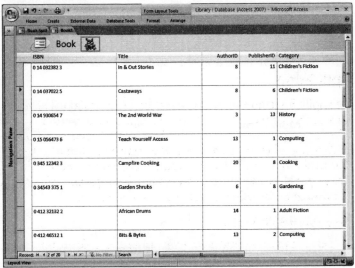

A split form (top) and multiple item form (below).

Multiple items form

A multiple items form is similar to Datasheet view, in that it shows several records at once, but you can customize the form by adding images and buttons if you wish.

To create a multiple items form:

1 Select the table that you want to create a form for in the Navigation panel.

Or

♦ Open the table in Datasheet view.

2 Click **Multiple Items** in the **Forms** group on the **Create** tab.

6.3 Form Wizard

The form types discussed above create forms using all the fields in the table or query on which they are based.

If you want to create a form using a subset of the fields available, or combine fields from more than one table, you could use the Form Wizard.

The wizard takes you through the forms design process step by step, asking you questions on the way.

We are going to design a form displaying the *ISBN*, *Title* and *Category* fields from the *Book* table, the *Author Name* details from the *Author* table and the *Publisher Name* from the *Publisher* table.

To create a form using Form Wizard:

1 Click **More Forms** in the **Forms** group on the **Create** tab.

2 Select **Form Wizard**.

3 At the **New Form** dialog box, choose **Form Wizard** and click **OK**.

4 At the first **Form Wizard** dialog box, select a table or query from which you want to include fields (you can include fields from more than one table or query on your form).

5 Choose the *Book* table and move the *ISBN*, *Title* and *Category* fields from the **Available fields list:** over into the Selected fields: list.

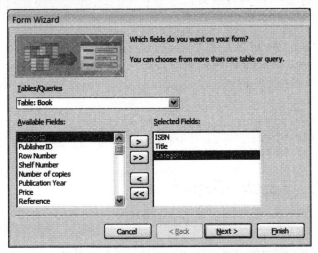

6 Select the *Author* table from the **Tables/Queries** list and add the *Firstname* and *Surname* fields.

7 Finally, select the *Publisher* table from the **Tables/Queries** list and add the *Company* field.

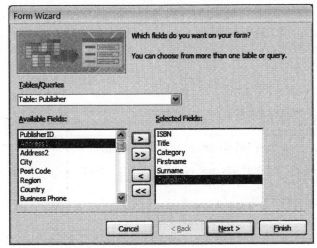

8 Now move on to the next step.

9 Select the option to use when viewing your data. In this example, choose **By Book**. Click **Next**.

10 Choose the layout you want to use for your form – **Columnar** in this example – and click **Next**.

11 At the next step you can choose the style of your forms. The style determines the colours and design layout. Pick one and move on to the next step.

12 When you reach the chequered flag you are at the last step in the wizard.

13 Give your form a name (either accept the one suggested or key in your own – this name will appear on the **Forms** list in the **Database** window).

14 Select **Open the form to view or enter information** and click **Finish**.

Your form should look something like this:

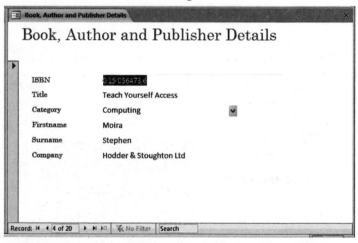

Working in a wizard

To move on to the next step: click [Next >]

To go back a step: click [< Back]

To exit the wizard without creating a form: click [Cancel]

To create a form using the default options: click [Finish]

You can move through the fields in your record using [Tab], and move between records using the navigation buttons at the bottom of the form.

When you close your form, you will find it on the **Forms** list in the **Database** window.

If you would like your data displayed in a summary form, e.g. a list of all the books you have from each publisher, the Form Wizard can easily help you design the form required for this.

Further work with a wizard

Work through the Form Wizard again selecting the following fields for your form. (You can include the *PublisherID* and/or *AuthorID* if you want to.)

Publisher table:	*Company*
Book table:	*ISBN*, *Title* and *Category Name*
Author table:	*Firstname* and *Surname*

1 When you get to the step where you are asked to select the option you want to use when viewing your data – choose **by Publisher**.

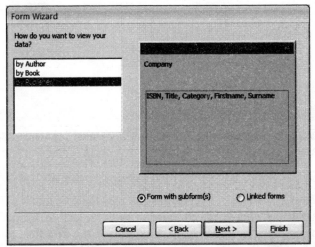

2 Select the **Form with subforms** option – the *Publisher* form will have a subform within it listing the book details.

3 At the next step choose the layout you want for your subform (tabular or datasheet).

4 Continue working through the Wizard, specifying the style and names you want to use for your forms (either accept the default ones, or amend them to your liking). These form names will be displayed in the Navigation pane.

5 At the chequered flag, choose **Open the form to view or enter information** and click **Finish**.

Two forms will be generated – your main form, the publisher one, and the book subform.

♦ Looking at your form you can use the lower set of navigation buttons to move from one publisher record to another.

♦ If you have a long list of books you can use the upper set of navigation buttons to move through the books in the list.

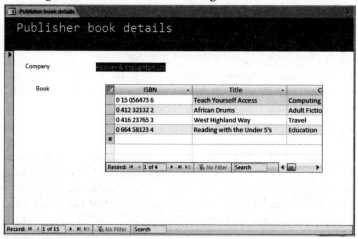

If you take the form through into Design view, you can see how this was set up.

The *PublisherID* (if included) and *Company* fields, are text boxes.

The lower section is a subform/subreport field. A subform field can display data from an existing table, query or form. The subform must be identified as the source of the data that will be displayed in that area of your main form. This is set up in the property options for that field.

- To view the property options, click on a *Subform* field to select it then click the **Property Sheet** button in the **Tools** group.

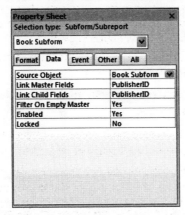

The subform/subreport property options are displayed in the Property Sheet panel. The **Data** tab shows the source of the data and the linking fields.

- Close the panel when you have finished.

6.4 Blank form

The blank form option can provide a quick way of creating a form, particularly if you only want to include a few fields. If you have users entering and editing the data you can simplify their view of the database by creating forms with just the fields they need, rather than giving them access to all the fields in a table or tables.

When you create a blank form, it is presented in Layout view.

To create a blank form:

1 Click ☐ Blank Form in the **Forms** group on the **Create** tab.

- A blank form is displayed in Layout view.

2 Drag the fields required from the **Field List** displayed on the right, onto the form.

- Not all fields can be dragged into all areas – if you cannot get the layout you require you might need to use the Form Wizard or Design view.

- Click the ⊞ and ⊟ buttons to the left of a table name to expand and collapse the field lists.

3 Add controls, e.g. Logo, Title, Data and Time as required (see section 6.5).

4 Save and close your form.

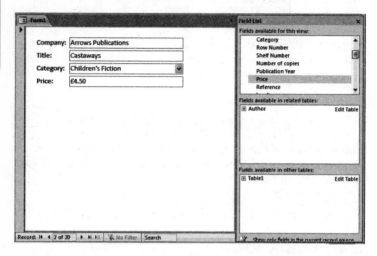

6.5 Adjusting controls in Layout view

You can resize, move and delete the controls in Layout view.

To resize a control:

1 Select it – click on it.

2 Move the pointer over the edge of the control – it becomes a double-headed arrow.

3 Click and drag to resize.

To move a control:

1 Select it.

2 Move the pointer inside the control – it becomes a 4-headed arrow when you are in a position to move the control.

3 Drag and drop to move it.

To delete a control:

1 Select it.

2 Press [Delete].

Form Layout tools

In Layout view, the Form Layout tools are displayed in the **Format** and **Arrange** tabs on the Ribbon. The most regularly used controls are in the **Controls** group on the **Format** tab. These allow you to add and format some controls in Layout view.

Logo

When you create a form or report, a standard logo is placed in the top left corner of the object as a placeholder. You can replace this with your own logo, or indeed any picture on your computer.

To add or replace a logo:

1 Click **Logo** in the **Controls** group on the **Format** tab.

2 Browse through your folders to locate and select the picture.

3 Resize the picture if necessary.

Other controls

To add or edit a title:

1 Click the **Title** button.

2 Insert or edit your text.

3 Click outside the title area.

To add a date or time control:

1 Click the **Date and Time** button.

2 Select **Include Date** and/or **Time**.

3 Choose the format.

4 Click **OK**.

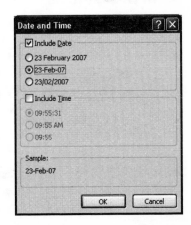

Line thickness, type and colour

To format the border of a control:

1 Click on a control on your form.

2 Select the line thickness, type and/or colour for the control border from the **Controls** group.

To change the properties of a control:

1 Select the control.

2 Click **Property Sheet** on the **Arrange** tab.

There will be many entries in the Property Sheet that you don't recognize or understand – don't worry about it. As you work with Access you will get to know the ones that you use.

6.6 Form Design

If you can't get exactly what you want using the other methods, Design view gives you access to all the controls and formatting options that are available for forms. We will design a simple form to display the Publisher details in Design view and use some of the features from Form Design when setting it up.

To create a new form in Design view:

• Click **Form Design** in the **Forms** group on the **Create** group.

Form Design tools

In Design view, the Form Design tools are displayed on the Ribbon, in two tabs, Design and Arrange. The groups of buttons specially for forms are shown below.

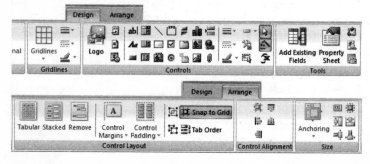

Rulers and Grid

If the Rulers and Grid are not displayed in Design view, click the buttons in the **Show/Hide** group on the **Arrange** tab to display them.

Rulers

Grid

Show/Hide

To make it easier to line up fields neatly on your form, make sure that the **Snap to Grid** command is switched on – in the **Control Layout** group on the **Arrange** tab.

Display the field lists

1 Click the **Add Existing Fields** button in the **Tools** group on the **Design** tab to display the **Field List** from your database. This has the tables that you can select fields from.

Add Existing Property
Fields Sheet

Tools

2 Expand the *Publisher* table field list – we will use this one.

Your screen should look like this:

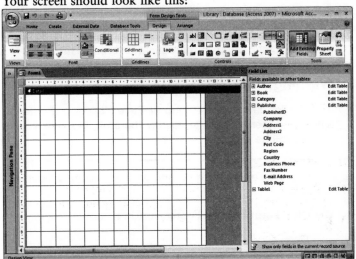

Form areas

The main areas in a form are the:

♦ **Detail** area

♦ **Form Header and Footer** area

♦ **Page Header and Footer** area.

The **Detail** area is the part of your form in which most of the detail from your table or query will be displayed.

The **Form Header** and **Footer** areas appear above and below the detail area for each record when you take your form back into Form view. They are used for titles or instructions you wish to appear above and below each form.

To toggle the display of the Form Header and Footer:

* Click the **Form Header/Footer** button in the **Show/Hide** group on the **Arrange** tab to display them or hide them again.

The **Page Headers** and **Footers** appear at the top and bottom of each page, should you opt to print your form. Page Headers would be used for main headings and column headings that you want to appear at the top of each printed page. The Page Footer is often used for page numbers, dates, or any other information you want to display at the foot of each page.

To toggle the display of the Page Header and Footer:

* Click the **Page Header/Footer** button in the **Show/Hide** group on the Arrange tab to display them or hide them again.

Warning!

If you enter data into the Form or Page Header or Footer areas, and then opt not to display the area, the data you entered will be lost.

In the form we are about to design, we need Form Header and Footer areas:

* Click the **Form Header/Footer** button to display them.

6.7 Labels

If you have instructions or headings to key into your form, you use the **Label** tool. We need a heading in our Form Header area – 'Book Publishers'.

* Labels are an example of unbound controls – they do not display information from your tables or queries.

1 Click the **Label** button 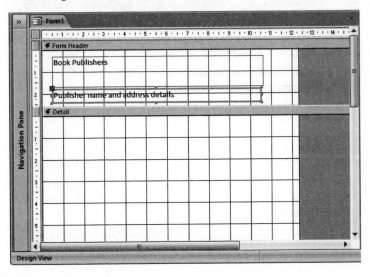 in the **Controls** group on the **Design** tab.

2 Move the mouse pointer into the form header area (notice the mouse pointer shape **+A**).

3 Click and drag in the **Form Header** area to draw a rectangle where you want your heading to go.

4 Let go of the mouse – the insertion point is inside the label field.

5 Key in your heading.

6 Click anywhere outside the label field.

Create another label underneath the one you have just made. This one should contain the text:

Publisher name and address details

If you think the Form Header area is not deep enough for this label, you can resize it by clicking and dragging the bottom edge of the header area (the pointer will change to a black double-headed arrow when you are in the correct place). The header area will also deepen automatically if you enter a label field too deep for its current size.

Your design should be similar to this:

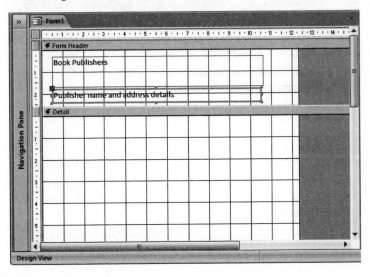

6.8 Formatting fields and controls

The fields you have added can be moved, resized, formatted or deleted – so it is not critical that you get everything right first time. To change the field attributes, you must select the field you want to work on.

◆ Click on the *Book Publishers* title to select it.

You will see that a selected field has handles around it – one in each corner and one half way along each side.

To format a control:

1 Click on it once to select it.

2 Use the buttons in the Font group on the Design tab to apply the formatting required.

3 Deselect the control.

Try making the *Book Publishers* heading font style Arial, font size 20, bold and text colour red! Now make the *Publisher name and address details* bold, italic and font size 12.

If the data is too large for the control, resize this as necessary. Your design should look something like the example below.

In the detail area of our form, we want to display the data held in the Publishers table – name, phone number, address, and so on.

- You can resize the **Detail** area by depth or width. Drag the bottom edge to deepen it, or the rightmost edge, to widen it.

6.9 Adding bound controls

To set up the design for the detail area we have to click and drag the fields required from the Field List onto the Detail area of our form. These fields are examples of *bound controls*. Once the fields are in the Detail area, we can position them, resize and format them as necessary. The fields we drag from the field list to the form are displayed as *text boxes*.

- Click and drag the *Company* field from the **Field List** and drop it on the detail area of your form.

You will notice that fields from the Field List consist of two parts – the leftmost part is the field label (either the field name or the caption if you entered one in the field properties), the rightmost part will display the actual data held in the field when you return to Form view.

Both components of the field are selected – if you move or delete the field the whole thing will be affected.

You can move either side of the field independently. Simply drag the large selection handle at the top left of each part when the field is selected.

- Place the *PublisherID* field next to the *Company* one. Your form should look similar to the one at the top of page 104.

- Format the label of each field (the left part) to be font size 10 and bold – click on the leftmost part to select it, then use the Formatting buttons to apply the formats required.

We are now ready to arrange the address details. This time, we want only one heading *Address* for all the individual address fields we will insert.

- Use the **Label** tool and enter a label that says 'Address' below the *Company* field.

Arranged under this, we want the *Address1*, *Address2*, *City*, *County*, *Postcode* and *Country* fields. As we already have an 'Address' label, we do not require the individual field labels – so we can delete them.

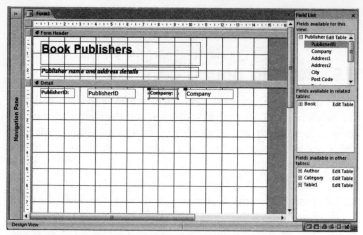

1 Click and drag your first field over – probably *Address1*. To delete the label (field name or caption), select the leftmost part of the field and press [**Delete**]. The label should disappear but the rightmost part should remain.

2 Do the same with the other address fields, and arrange them attractively on your form.

3 Insert the *Phone, Fax, e-mail and Website* fields to the right of the address (use labels as you wish to enhance the layout).

4 We don't need the Form Footer area on this form – click and drag its bottom edge up until it disappears.

Your form should be similar to the one below.

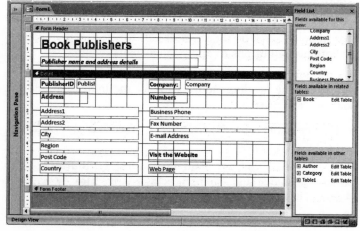

5 Click the **Save** button. At the **Save As** dialog box, give your form a suitable name and click **OK**.

6 Take your form through into Form view to see how it looks. It should be similar to the one below.

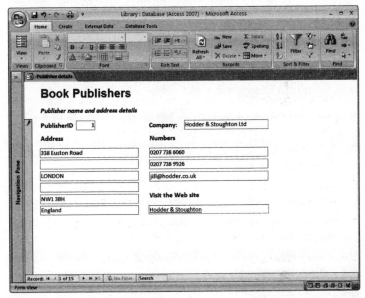

When you close your form, you will find its name displayed on the Forms list in the Navigation pane.

Control Wizard

Before you start experimenting with the following controls, ensure that the Control Wizard is switched on. The button for the Wizard is in the Controls group on the Design tab. When the wizard is on, you can work through it each time you add a control to your form, making it much easier to set things up the way you want them.

6.10   Combo boxes and list boxes

Combo boxes and list boxes can be used when you have a limited set of options to choose from. Using them can help ensure accurate data entry as the user can select the entry rather than type it in. When you specify a *LookUp* field in the data type of a table a combo box is created automatically in the table and when you add the field to a form.

We could use a combo box or a list box for the *Country* field in the *Publishers* details form. The publishers that we deal with are all from England, Scotland and the USA.

Combo box

To insert a combo box field for *Country*, take the Publisher details form into Design view and delete the *Country* field.

1 Click the **Combo box** button [▦] in the **Controls** group.

2 Drag the field that you wish to use from the field list onto your form – *Country* in this example.

3 Select *I will type in the values that I want* and click **Next**.

4 Specify the number of columns – we only need one.

5 Enter the possible values for the combo box – 'England', 'Scotland' and 'USA'.

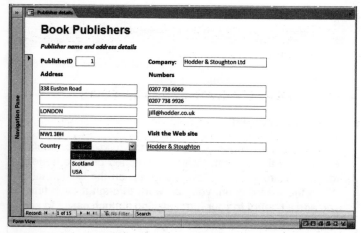

A combo box in use – if the required data is not in the list, a user can type it in.

6 Drag the edge of the column to set its width and click **Next**.

7 Select the field to store the combo box value in – *Country* should be suggested – and click **Next**.

8 Give the Combo box a label – accept the default or set your own.

9 Click **Finish**.

10 Resize and position the combo box as needed.

List boxes

List boxes are set up in exactly the same way as a combo box, just start with the **List box** button 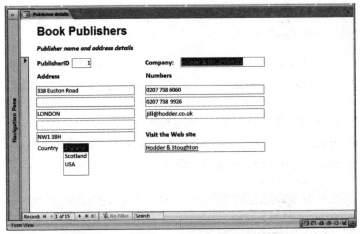 in the **Controls** group.

A list box only allows users to pick from a fixed list of items.

6.11 Checkboxes and buttons

If you simply drag a Yes/No field onto a form, it will be displayed as a checkbox, but Yes/No fields can also be displayed as toggle buttons or option buttons. It is conventional to use these for Yes/No indicators. Option buttons are normally associated with groups of options, from which only one can be selected.

To display a Yes/No field as a toggle button:

1 Click the **Toggle** button ![toggle icon] in the **Controls** group.

2 Drag the field from the field list onto your form.

3 With the field selected, click the **Property Sheet** button and enter a suitable caption for the button.

Property Sheet

4 Close the **Properties** dialog box.

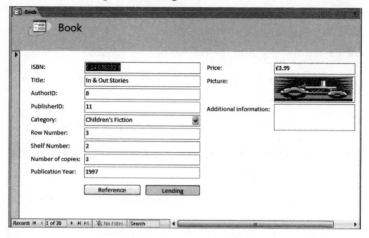

To display a Yes/No field as an option button:

1 Click the **Option button** in the **Controls** group.

2 Drag the field from the field list onto your form and position it as required.

6.12 Option group

Option groups are useful when you have a limited number of options, from which you can select one. We could use a group for the *Shelf Number* in the *Book* form. Open the *Book* form in Design view and delete the *Shelf Number* field (you might want to rearrange some of the fields to make room for the group).

1 Click the **Option group** button in the **Controls** group.

2 Drag the field from the field list onto the form.

♦ Work through the wizard, clicking **Next** after each step.

3 Insert the **Label name** for each option button.

4 Specify the default choice if you wish.

5 Edit the **Values** if necessary – these will be stored in the underlying table.

6 Indicate the field where the value will be stored.

7 Set the display options.

8 Edit the Option group caption if necessary.

9 Click **Finish**.

10 Move/resize the Option group as required.

Calculations

You can perform calculations on a form, as in queries, using the operators + (add), - (minus), * (multiply) and / (divide). Calculations must be placed in a text box.

1 Create a text box on your form.

2 Replace the left-hand side text with the label you want your field to have.

3 Enter the formula required in the right-hand side.

4 Format the right-hand side as required, e.g. currency, decimal places (in the Property options for the field).

5 Go into Form view to see the results.

♦ **Formulas** start with '=' and are enclosed within parentheses ( ). Use the following **operators** within the formulas: +, -, /, *. (See section 7.12.)

♦ **Field names** in formulas are put in square brackets [ ].

6.13 Inserting images

You can easily insert an image onto a form (or report).

1 Display the form area that you want the image on.

2 Click the **Image** button  in the **Controls** group.

3 Drag on the form to set the size and position for the image.

4 Locate the picture (browse through your drives and folders).

5 Move/resize the image as required.

Size mode

You may need to set the size mode to get a good fit.

To set the size mode:

1 Display the **Property Sheet** for the image.

2 Locate the **Size mode** property – on the **Format** or **All** tabs.

3 Set it to **Zoom** or **Stretch** – whichever gives the best effect.

4 Close the **Property Sheet**.

Property Sheet	✕
Selection type: Image	
Image46	
Format	Data	Event	Other	All	
Visible	Yes
Picture	AN00790 .WMF
Picture Tiling	No
Size Mode	Zoom
Picture Alignment	Center
Picture Type	Embedded
Width	2cm
Height	1.7cm
Top	0.199cm
Left	6.099cm
Back Style	Transparent
Back Color	#FFFFFF
Border Style	Transparent
Border Width	Hairline
Border Color	#000000
Special Effect	Flat
Hyperlink Address	
Hyperlink SubAddress	
Gridline Style Top	Transparent
Gridline Style Bottom	Transparent
Gridline Style Left	Transparent
Gridline Style Right	Transparent
Gridline Color	#000000
Gridline Width Top	1 pt
Gridline Width Bottom	1 pt
Gridline Width Left	1 pt

6.14 Command buttons

Command buttons perform actions such as printing a form, opening a report or applying a filter. We could add a command button to the Library Books form to print the form.

1 Click the **Button control** 🔳 in the **Controls** group.

2 Click on your form to set the position for the control.

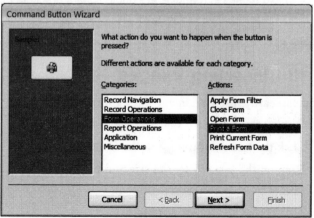

3 Select the **Category**, e.g. *Form Operations* and the **Action**, e.g. *Print a Form* in the Command Button Wizard dialog box and click **Next**.

4 Work through the steps of the Wizard, setting the options as required and click **Finish**.

See Chapter 12 for more information on macros.

6.15 Tab control

Some forms contain many fields and/or text, e.g. instructions. With these you can use separate pages in the Tab control to display different areas of the information on your form.

1 Click the **Tab control** button ▥ in the **Controls** group.

2 Click and drag in the Detail area to place the Tab control.

3 Add the fields required on Page 1.

4 Select the Page 2 tab and add its fields.

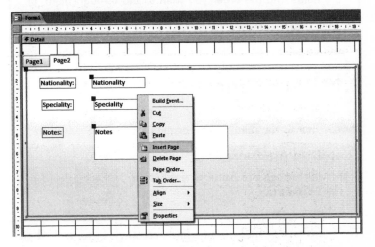

To **add or delete pages:**

1 Click on the tab of the page you wish to insert after, or display the page to delete.

2 Right-click on the field and select **Insert page** or **Delete page** as required.

To change page order:

1 Right-click on the field and click **Page Order...**

2 Select the page and click **Move Up** or **Move Down** as necessary.

♦ Pages can be renamed by editing the **Name** on the **Other** tab of their **Properties** sheet.

Tab order

When designing a form you will probably move your fields around and change their order several times before you are finally satisfied with the form layout. As a result of this, you may find that when you press [Tab] to move from field to field in Form view, you jump around all over the place. When this happens, you should reset the Tab order to give a more logical progression through the form.

In Design view, select Tab Order from the View menu. Drag the fields into the order you wish to tab through them, or Select Auto Order to tab through them in the order that they appear on the form.

6.16 AutoFormat

As an alternative to formatting your form manually, you could choose one of the many AutoFormats.

To apply an AutoFormat:

1 Scroll through the **AutoFormat** list on the **Format** tab.

2 Select a format.

The font, background colours, lines, rectangles, etc. will all pick up the formats included within the set you choose.

At the bottom of the AutoFormat gallery you will find the **AutoFormat Wizard....** This option allows you to control which formatting options – font, border or colour, etc. – are applied to your form.

6.17 Printing forms

Forms are usually used for data entry and edit. There may be times when you want to print them out – or you could perhaps print out an empty form to send to someone for manual completion.

If you do want to print out a form, you can do so using similar techniques to those used when printing out a datasheet.

1 Open the form in Form view.

2 Display the form that you want to print.

3 Click the Microsoft Office button.

4 Click **Print** to display the **Print** dialog box.

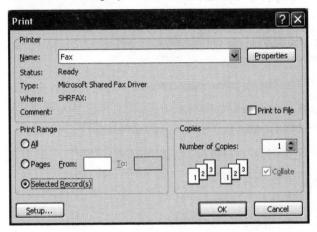

5 Choose **Selected Record(s)** in the **Print what** options.

6 Click **OK**.

Alternatively, you could add a command button (see section 6.14) with the category *Record operations* and the action *Print Record*.

Summary

In this chapter we have considered various ways in which you can set up forms in your database. We have discussed:

+ Form controls – bound, unbound and calculated

+ Form views – Form, Layout and Design

+ Using the form tools to create forms

+ Setting up a form using the Form Wizard

+ Starting from a blank form

+ Adjusting controls

+ Working in Form Design

+ Form Headers and Footers

+ Labels

+ Formatting fields and controls

+ Combo and List boxes

+ Checkboxes and buttons in your forms

+ Setting up option groups using the Wizard

+ Inserting images

+ Command buttons

+ The Tab order on forms

+ AutoFormat

+ Printing forms.

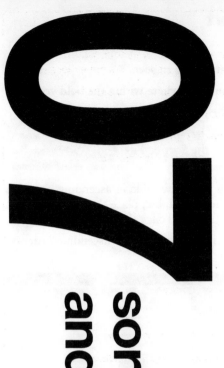

07 sort, filter and query

In this chapter you will learn:

- about simple and multi-level sorts
- how to find data
- about filtering records from tables
- about select and parameter queries
- about calculations in queries

7.1 Simple sort

It is very easy to sort the records in your table on a single field.

1 Open the table you are going to sort.

2 Place the insertion point anywhere within the field you want to sort the records on.

3 Click the **Sort Ascending** [↓] or **Sort Descending** [↓] button in the **Sort & Filter** group on the **Home** tab.

* To sort the records in the *Book* table in ascending order on the *Title* field, open the *Book* table, place the insertion point anywhere in the *Title* field, and click the **Sort Ascending** tool.

The *Book* table, with the records sorted into ascending order on the *Title* field, is displayed below.

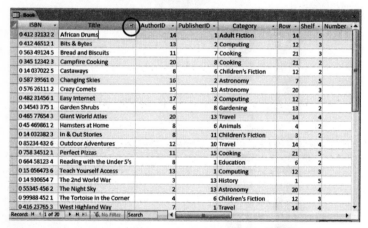

ISBN	Title	AuthorID	PublisherID	Category	Row	Shelf	Number
0 412 32132 2	African Drums	14	1	Adult Fiction	14	5	
0 412 46512 1	Bits & Bytes	13	2	Computing	12	3	
0 563 49124 5	Bread and Biscuits	11	7	Cooking	21	3	
0 345 12342 3	Campfire Cooking	20	8	Cooking	21	2	
0 14 037022 5	Castaways	8	6	Children's Fiction	12	2	
0 587 39561 0	Changing Skies	16	2	Astronomy	7	5	
0 576 26111 2	Crazy Comets	15	13	Astronomy	20	3	
0 482 31456 1	Easy Internet	17	2	Computing	12	2	
0 34543 375 1	Garden Shrubs	6	8	Gardening	13	2	
0 465 77654 3	Giant World Atlas	20	13	Travel	14	4	
0 45 469861 2	Hamsters at Home	8	6	Animals	4	2	
0 14 032382 3	In & Out Stories	8	11	Children's Fiction	3	2	
0 85234 432 6	Outdoor Adventures	12	10	Travel	14	4	
0 758 34512 1	Perfect Pizzas	11	15	Cooking	21	5	
0 664 58123 4	Reading with the Under 5's	8	1	Education	6	2	
0 15 056473 6	Teach Yourself Access	13	1	Computing	12	3	
0 14 930654 7	The 2nd World War	3	13	History	1	5	
0 55345 456 2	The Night Sky	2	13	Astronomy	20	4	
0 99988 452 1	The Tortoise in the Corner	4	6	Children's Fiction	12	3	
0 416 23765 3	West Highland Way	7	1	Travel	14	4	

Record: 1 of 20   No Filter   Search

Notice the arrow to the right of the name in the *Title* column – showing that the column has been sorted into ascending order.

* To clear a sort, click the **Clear All Sorts** button [↓] in the **Sort & Filter** group.

Saving changes

When you close a table that you have sorted, you will be asked if you want to save the changes.

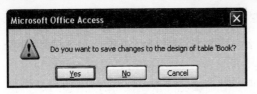

To save the records in the new, sorted order, choose **Yes**.

7.2 Multi-level sort

You can use the Sort command buttons to sort your data on more than one field if you wish.

Let's say we wanted to sort the *Publisher* table so that the *Country* names were in ascending order, then within each country the *City* entries were in ascending order, and where there was more than one publisher in a city, the *Company* names were in descending order.

To perform this sort, start with the lowest level sort first – the Company names.

1 Click in the *Company* field and click the **Sort Descending** button.

2 Click in the *Town* field and click the **Sort Ascending** button.

3 Click in the *Country* field and sort it into ascending order.

PublisherID	Company	Address1	Add	City	PostCode	Count	Country	Business
13	Outreach College Press	Wilson Way West		LIVERPOO	LP3		England	
3	Westward Lock Ltd	18 Clifftop Street		LONDON	W1X 1RB		England	0207 333 4
15	Trueform Press Ltd	Manderson House	8 Geor	LONDON	SW3 6RB		England	0207 334 3
11	Scrambler Publications Lt	6-9 Prince Street		LONDON	NW1 0AE		England	0208 556 4
1	Hodder & Stoughton Ltd	338 Euston Road		LONDON	NW1 3BH		England	0207 738 6
7	Harry Cousin Ltd	10-23 Frosty Road	South I	LONDON	W6 8JB		England	0208 444 6
9	Darling Kinghorn	2 Herbert Street		LONDON	WC2E 8PS		England	0208 665 7
14	Carling & Sons plc	4 St Thomas' Park		LONDON	SW1		England	
8	Beaver Books Ltd	7 Squirrel Lane		LONDON	W8 5TZ		England	0207 445 7
6	Arrows Publications	Randall House	1 Cava	LONDON	SW1V 2SA		England	0207 443 5
12	BPU Publications	Europa House	Queen	OXFORD		Oxfords	England	
2	Borthwick-Henderson	Applewood Hous	Apple	OXFORD	OX1 7DP	Oxfords	England	01865 335
10	City Publications Ltd	7 Queen Street		EDINBURG	EH1 3UG	Midloth	Scotland	0131 445 6
5	Christy Corporation	20 E 103rd Street		INDIANAP	46290		USA	
4	Softcell Press	1 Softcell rise		ORLANDO	33412-6641	Florida	USA	
(New)								

Record: 14 4 5 of 15 ▶ ▶ ▶ No Filter Search

If you look carefully at the result, you should see that the countries are in ascending order. Where there are several towns in one country those towns are in ascending order, e.g. in England, the towns are Liverpool, London and then Oxford. Where there is more than one publisher in a town, the company names are in descending order. In London we have Westward Lock Ltd, Trueform Press Ltd, Scrambler Publications Ltd, Hodder & Stoughton Ltd, etc.

• Experiment with the sort feature on your tables until you are sure that you see how it works.

If you sort your records, and then decide that you want to keep them in the new order, save your table before you close it.

7.3 Find

To locate a record in your table, you can use the navigation buttons at the bottom of your datasheet or form, or go to a specific record by typing its number in the number field within the navigation buttons and pressing [**Enter**].

If you have a lot of records in your table, the Find function can provide a quick way of locating a specific record.

Try locating a book in a particular category:

1 Place the insertion point anywhere within the *Category* field in the *Book* table.

2 Click the **Find** button in the **Find** group.

3 At the **Find** dialog box, enter the detail you are looking for – *Cooking* in this example.

4 Edit the other fields as necessary.

5 Click **Find Next** to start the search or look for another match.

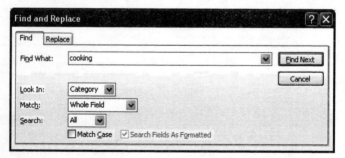

6 Close the dialog box once you have found your record.

7.4 Filter

There will be times when you want to display a specific group of records from your table – a list of American authors, or authors who specialize in travel books for example. This is done by **filtering** the records. You can filter your records by **Selection** or by **Form**.

Filter by selection

Try filtering the *Author* table to display those that are (or are not) of a specific nationality.

1 Open the *Author* table.

2 Position the insertion point in the field of a record that has the criterion that you are looking for, e.g. to filter for American authors, set the insertion point within the *Nationality* field, in a record where the author is American.

3 Click the **Selection** button.

4 Select an option – Equals, Does Not Equal, Contains or Does Not Contain.

> Selection ▾
>
> **Equals "American"**
> **Does Not Equal "American"**
> **Contains "American"**
> **Does Not Contain "American"**

5 You can filter a filtered list using the same technique, narrowing down your list of records as you go, e.g. to display those that specialize in travel books (or those who don't).

This list displays those who are not American, but do write travel books.

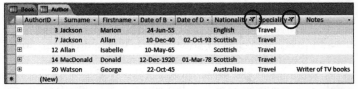

Note the indicators at the top of the columns that have been filtered.

* To remove the filter, click the **Toggle Filter** button in the Sort & Filter group.

> ▼
> Filter
> Selection ▾
> Advanced ▾
> Toggle Filter
> Sort & Filter

You can also filter your records by selecting options from the filter list.

To specify a selection:

1 Click in the column you want to base your selection on.

2 Click **Filter** in the **Sort & Filter** group.

Or

♦ Click the arrow to the right of the field name you want to filter by.

3 Deselect the **Select All** checkbox.

4 Tick the checkboxes to set the criteria for your selection.

5 Click **OK**.

To clear your selection:

♦ Click the **Toggle Filter** button in the **Sort & Filter** group.

Or

1 Click the arrow to the right of the field name.

2 Choose **Clear filter from...** from the list.

Filter by form

An alternative to filtering your data based on selections, is to use a form layout to specify your criteria. When filtering by form, you can specify different sets of criteria and apply them all at the same time. For example, you might want to list all the books published on Astronomy and Computing in 2002.

1 Open the *Books* table.

2 Click **Advanced** in the **Sort & Filter** group, and then choose **Filter by Form**.

3 Use the drop-down lists at each field to set your criteria.

4 Set up each set of criteria on a new tab – bottom left of the window.

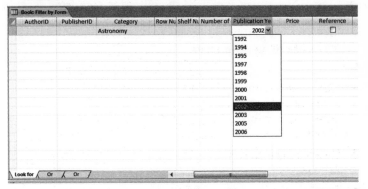

5 Click **Toggle Filter** once you have all your criteria set up. The results will be displayed.

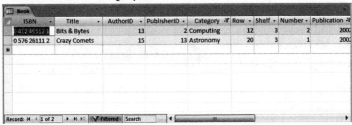

♦ Click **Toggle Filter** to display all records again.

To reapply the filter:

♦ Click **Advanced**, and then **Apply Filter/Sort**.

To clear the filter:

♦ Click **Advanced**, and then **Clear All Filters**.

Query Design

Filtering and sorting can be achieved quickly and easily using the methods discussed above. However, the Query Design feature gives you many more options. The topics discussed in the remainder of this chapter are in the context of using the Query Design feature.

7.5 Query Design

In the examples so far, we have sorted and filtered records within one table. Sometimes you need to collect the data from several tables, and sort or filter it, or you may not want to display all of the fields from a table in the result. In these situations, you might find it easier to work in Query Design.

We will set up a query to display Book Title, Author, Publisher and Year Published data.

♦ If you have a table open, close it.

To set up a query in Design view:

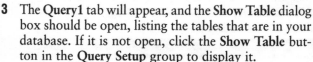

1 Display the **Create** tab on the Ribbon.

2 Click **Query Design** in the **Other** group.

3 The **Query1** tab will appear, and the **Show Table** dialog box should be open, listing the tables that are in your database. If it is not open, click the **Show Table** button in the **Query Setup** group to display it.

4 Add the *Author*, *Book* and *Publisher* tables to the **Query** tab.

5 Close the **Show Table** dialog box.

♦ If you add a table by mistake, or decide you don't need one that you have added, select it in the upper pane (see opposite) and press [Delete] to remove it.

Selection techniques in the Show Table dialog box

♦ **To select one table:** click on it.

♦ **To select several adjacent tables:** click on the first one and then hold down [Shift] and click on the last one.

♦ **To select several non-adjacent tables:** hold down [Ctrl] and click on each of the tables you want.

The query tab will be displayed, with the Query Design tools in the Ribbon. The tables are displayed in the upper pane and the query grid is in the lower pane.

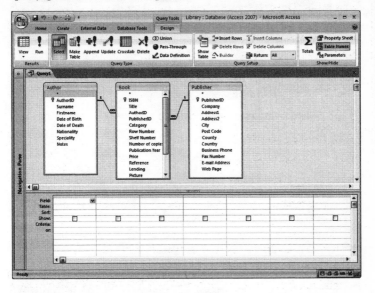

Adding fields to the query grid

The next step is adding the fields that you want displayed when you run your query, to the query grid.

To add fields to the query grid:

◆ Double-click on the field in the table in the upper pane.

You should add the:

> *Title* and *Publication Year* from the *Book* table
>
> *Surname* and *Firstname* from the *Author* table
>
> *Company* from the *Publisher* table.

Things to note in the lower pane:

◆ **Table** row indicates which table the field has been taken from.

◆ **Show** indicates whether or not a field will be displayed when you display the results – a tick means that it will show.

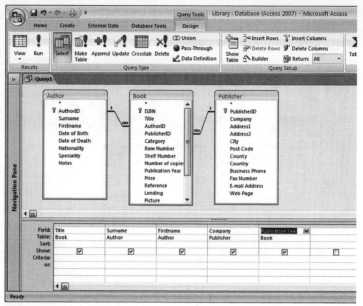

Running the query

Once you have your query set up, you have to run it to display the results.

To display your results:

* Click **Run** in the **Results** group within the **Query Tools** Design tab.

Title	Surname	Firstname	Company	Publication
In & Out Stories	Smith	Dick	Scrambler Publications Lt	1997
Castaways	Smith	Dick	Arrows Publications	1994
The 2nd World War	Jackson	Marion	Outreach College Press	1998
Teach Yourself Access 2003	Stephen	Moira	Hodder & Stoughton Ltd	2003
Campfire Cooking	Watson	George	Beaver Books Ltd	1995
Garden Shrubs	Ferguson	John	Beaver Books Ltd	2006
African Drums	MacDonald	Donald	Hodder & Stoughton Ltd	1992
Bits & Bytes	Stephen	Moira	Borthwick-Henderson	2002
West Highland Way	Jackson	Allan	Hodder & Stoughton Ltd	2002
Hamsters at Home	Smith	Dick	Arrows Publications	1999
Giant World Atlas	Watson	George	Outreach College Press	2002
Easy Internet	Ferguson	Alan	Borthwick-Henderson	2006
The Night Sky	McDonald	Alestair	Outreach College Press	2001
Bread and Biscuits	Meunier	Luc	Harry Cousin Ltd	1997
Crazy Comets	Williams	Peter	Outreach College Press	2002
Changing Skies	Borthwick	Anne	Borthwick-Henderson	2000
Reading with the Under 5's	Smith	Dick	Hodder & Stoughton Ltd	2005

Record: ◄ ◄ 3 of 20 ► ►► No Filter Search

When your results are displayed, you can return to the Query design by clicking the View command button or by selecting Design view from the view options.

The selected fields from all your records are displayed in the result.

Save your query:

1 Click the **Save** tool on the Quick Access toolbar.

2 Give it a name that reflects the nature of the query.

♦ Close the query – it will be displayed in the Navigation panel.

Notice that it is displayed under each of the three tables that it takes its data from – *Book, Publisher* and *Author*.

To open a query again and display the results:

♦ Double-click on it in the Navigation pane.

Or

♦ Right-click on it and choose **Open**.

To open a query in Design view:

♦ Right-click on it and choose **Design view**.

As you work through the following examples, save any queries that you want to keep.

7.6 Select queries

If you want a subset of your records, you can specify in Query Design the criteria you want to select on. The criteria are specified through expressions that you key into the criteria rows. When entering expressions there are one or two rules you should keep in mind.

If you want to look for multiple criteria within the same record, the criteria are entered on the same row. If you wanted a list of all the books published by Hodder & Stoughton, you would enter 'Hodder & Stoughton Ltd' in the *Company* column in the criteria row.

However, if you wanted a list of all the books published by Hodder & Stoughton Ltd in 1992, you would enter 'Hodder & Stoughton Ltd' in the *Company* column and '1992' in the *Publication Year* column on the same criteria row.

When you enter criteria in different cells in the same row, Access uses the **And** operator. It looks for all the conditions being met before returning the record details. If you enter criteria in cells in different criteria rows, Access uses the **Or** operator.

Experiment with different criteria using your tables.

1 Create a new query using Query Design.
2 Add the *Book*, *Author* and *Publisher* tables to the **Select Query** tab.
3 Select the fields you want, in the order you want them to appear – use the same ones as in the previous example:

• *Title* and *Publication Year* from the *Book* table
• *Surname* and *Firstname* from the *Author* table
• *Company* from the *Publisher* table.

7.7 Or conditions

This time, we want our books in ascending order on the Title field, but we only want to show the books we have from the publishers Hodder & Stoughton Ltd and those from Borthwick-Henderson Ltd. We have also decided not to display the details in the Publication Year column.

1 Set the sort order required in the *Title* column

2 In the *Company* column, enter 'Hodder & Stoughton Ltd' in the first criteria row and 'Borthwick-Henderson Ltd' in the next criteria row – Access will return records that have **Hodder & Stoughton Ltd** OR **Borthwick-Henderson Ltd** in the *Company* field.

3 Deselect the **Show** checkbox in the *Publication Year* column as we do not want this column displayed in the result.

4 Run your query and note the results.

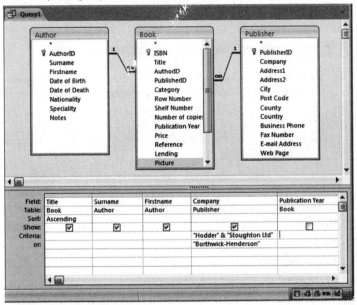

The book titles should be in ascending order, the author name and publisher name are displayed – but only for the publishers specified in the criteria rows. The year of publication is not displayed.

Title	Surname	Firstname	Company
African Drums	MacDonald	Donald	Hodder & Stoughton Ltd
Bits & Bytes	Stephen	Moira	Borthwick-Henderson
Changing Skies	Borthwick	Anne	Borthwick-Henderson
Easy Internet	Ferguson	Alan	Borthwick-Henderson
Reading with the Under 5's	Smith	Dick	Hodder & Stoughton Ltd
Teach Yourself Access 2003	Stephen	Moira	Hodder & Stoughton Ltd
West Highland Way	Jackson	Allan	Hodder & Stoughton Ltd

Record: 1 of 7   No Filter   Search

7.8 And conditions

This time try to get a list of all the books published by Hodder & Stoughton Ltd in 1992.

1 Enter 'Hodder & Stoughton Ltd' in the *Company* and '1992' in the *Publication Year* column of the first criteria row.

2 Run your query.

Access will return details for records where both criteria are met in the same record – those with 'Hodder & Stoughton Ltd' in the *Company* field AND '1992' in the *Publication Year* column.

7.9 Comparison operators

When you enter an expression in the **Criteria** row, as in the examples in sections 7.7 and 7.8, Access assumes that you mean to use the comparison operator =, i.e. you are looking for records where the text or value in the corresponding field in the datasheet is equal to the text or value that you have entered in the **Criteria** row in the **Query Design** grid.

There will be times when you wish to extract records using different comparison operators. If you don't mean 'equals' you must enter the appropriate operator into your expression in the Criteria row.

You can identify the range required using the following operators:

<	Less than
>	More than
<=	Less than or equal to
>=	More than or equal to
<>	Not equal to
Between…And…	Between the first and the last value entered (including the values)

To get a list of books by authors whose surname began with the letter 'M' through to the end of the alphabet, you would enter '>=M' in the criteria row of the *Surname* column.

If you want a list of books published before 1994, you would enter '<1994' in the criteria row in the *Publication Year* column.

To get a list of all the books published in 1992, 1993, 1994, 1995 and 1996 you would enter 'Between 1992 And 1996' in the criteria row of the *Publication Year* column.

The on-line Help will give you other examples of expressions you can experiment with.

7.10 Wild card characters

When specifying your criteria you can use 'wild card' characters to represent either individual characters or a string of characters. The wild card characters are:

* *   which can be used to represent a string of characters, or

* ?   which can be used to represent a single character.

For example, if you wanted a list of all the publishers in your database with a postcode of NW1 you could use the * wild card to represent the second part of the postcode so that its detail didn't matter.

Enter 'NW1*' into the criteria row for the PostCode field. When you leave the cell, the 'NW1*' changes to read 'Like "NW1*"'. All records that have a postcode beginning with NW1 will be returned when you run the query.

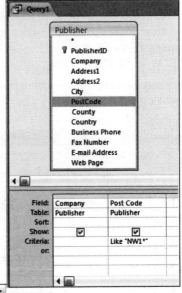

If you wanted a list of all books that had 'Cooking' in the title, but sometimes the word appeared at the beginning, e.g. *Cooking for Kids*, or in the middle, e.g. *Indian Cooking for Beginners*

or at the end, e.g. *Party Cooking*, the wild cards can help you get a complete list. Entering *Cooking* in the criteria row would do the trick!

Single letters that may vary can be represented using '?'. If you wanted to find a particular author in your list, but you couldn't remember whether the surname was Wilson or Wilton, you could enter *Wil?on* in the criteria row.

7.11 Parameter queries

There may be times when you run the same query regularly, but you need to change the criteria each time. Instead of entering the criteria into the Design view for the query, you can enter a *prompt* that will appear on the screen requesting your input each time you run the query.

You could set up a query to list the books written by a specific author with a prompt to ask for the author name each time the query is run.

1 In the criteria row, in the *Surname* column enter the prompt you wish to appear when the query is run: '[Enter Surname]'

2 Enter a prompt in the *Firstname* column: '[Enter Firstname]'

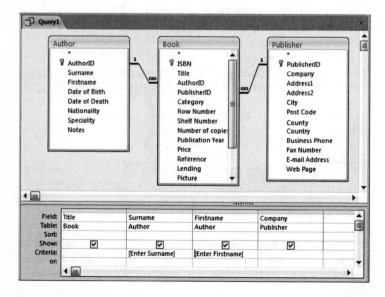

The prompts must be included within [**square brackets**], and cannot consist of just the field name, although the field name may be included within the prompt – '[Surname]' won't work, but '[Enter Surname]' will!

3 Run the query.

4 Enter the *Surname*, and click **OK**.

5 Likewise, enter the *Firstname*, and click **OK**.

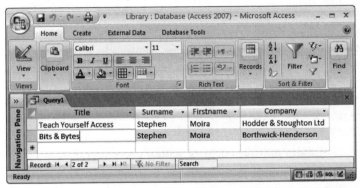

The results will be displayed on your screen.

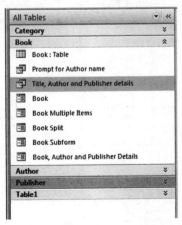

6 Save this Query – you could call it *Prompt for author name*.

You will find the queries you have saved listed in the Navigation pane.

- To run a query from the Navigation pane, double-click on the query name, or right-click on it and select **Open**.

- To open a query in Design view, right-click on it and choose **Design view**.

7.12 Calculations

There may be times when you need to carry out calculations on your data. Calculations cannot be performed in a table, but they can be performed in a query. Let's say you wanted to calculate how much money had been spent on each title in your library.

In the *Book* table we have recorded the price of each book and also the number of copies we have in the library. To find out how much we have spent on each title we would need to multiply the value in the *Price* field by the value in the *Number of copies* field.

Rules for calculated fields in queries:

◆ Calculated field names must be followed by a : (colon), then by the expression to perform the calculation.

◆ Field names must be enclosed within square brackets [ ].

◆ Operators used to perform calculations are + (add), – (subtract), * (multiply), / (divide).

◆ Formulas must be enclosed within parentheses ( ).

To enter a formula to calculate the amount spent on each title:

1 Add the fields required to the **Query Design** grid – I have added *Category*, *Title*, *Price* and *Number of copies*.

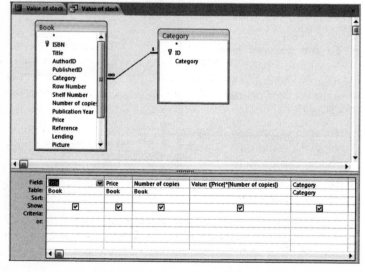

2   In the next column in the query grid, add a field name for the calculated field – just type it in (in this example I have typed in *Value*) – followed by a colon :

3   In the same cell, enter the formula to calculate the value, e.g. ([Price]*[No of copies])

4   Run the query and check that your calculations are correct.

◆   Save this query (you can simply call it *Value of stock*) so that you can use it in the report in section 8.5.

Title	Price	Number	Value
In & Out Stories	£3.99	3	£11.97
Castaways	£4.50	2	£9.00
The 2nd World War	£12.50	3	£37.50
Teach Yourself Access	£8.99	2	£17.98
Campfire Cooking	£4.99	1	£4.99
Garden Shrubs	£4.99	2	£9.98
African Drums	£12.50	1	£12.50
Bits & Bytes	£9.99	2	£19.98
West Highland Way	£12.50	1	£12.50
Hamsters at Home	£4.50	1	£4.50
Giant World Atlas	£35.00	1	£35.00
Easy Internet	£9.99	2	£19.98
The Night Sky	£35.00	2	£70.00
Bread and Biscuits	£12.50	2	£25.00
Crazy Comets	£17.50	1	£17.50
Changing Skies	£10.99	2	£21.98
Reading with the Under 5's	£6.99	2	£13.98
Perfect Pizzas	£9.99	2	£19.98
Outdoor Adventures	£15.00	2	£30.00
The Tortoise in the Corner	£6.50	2	£13.00

Record: 1 of 20   No Filter   Search

You can also perform a different type of calculation in a query. These are called *aggregate* functions, e.g. sum, avg, min, max and count. An aggregate function produces summary information from your data.

You could use this type of function to work out how many books you had in your library. You must add another row to the **Query Design** grid for this function – the **Total** row.

1   To display this row, click the **Totals** button on the **Query Design** tab.

2   To calculate the total number of books in your library, add the *Number of copies* field to the **Query Design** grid then choose **SUM** from the options in the **Total** row.

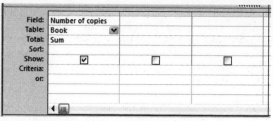

3 Run the query to find out the answer.

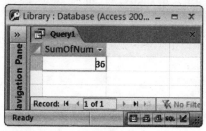

You could use a similar query to find out how many books you had in each category. Add the *Category* field to the **Query Design** grid, and choose **Group By** in the **Total** row for this field. If you want the results sorted, e.g. in ascending number of copies, set the sort order.

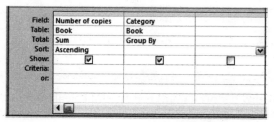

♦ Run the query and check the results.

Experiment – it is one of the best ways to get good at this!

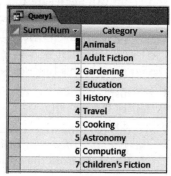

7.13 Date( ) function and calculation

The Date() function returns the current date from your computer system as a number. Date calculations are done in *days*. You will have to convert the days to weeks (/7) or years (/365) as required.

In the *Library* database the Date function could be used in a query to calculate the age of the authors. In other situations it could be used to calculate the length of service of an employee, or the length of time an item has been in stock.

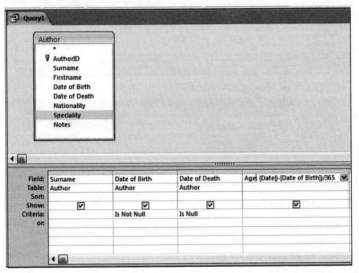

In this example the **Is Null** and **Is Not Null** criteria are used (see 7.14) to select the authors that are still alive, then the Date function is used in the calculation.

The result will display with several decimal places unless you format the *Age* field to **Fixed**, with 0 decimal places.

To format the *Age* field, click the **Properties** tool when the insertion point is in the field and set the properties in the dialog box.

Property Sheet	✕
Selection type: Field Properties	
General Lookup	
Description	
Format	Fixed
Decimal Places	0
Input Mask	
Caption	
Smart Tags	

7.14 Is Null/Is Not Null

You can use a query to help you locate records that have an empty field (or don't have an empty field). For example, you could use a query to display all the Publisher records that you don't have an e-mail address for.

- To check for an empty field, you use the criterion **Is Null**.
- To check that a field is not empty, use **Is Not Null**.

Field:	Company	City	Business Phone	E-mail Address
Table:	Publisher	Publisher	Publisher	Publisher
Sort:				
Show:	☑	☑	☑	☑
Criteria:				Is Null
or:				

The results of this query will be:

Company	City	Business Ph	E-mail Address
Beaver Books Ltd	LONDON	0207 445 7000	
Scrambler Publications Lt	LONDON	0208 556 4354	

Summary

In this chapter we have covered how to sort data, extract records that meet specific criteria and perform calculations. You have learnt how to:

- Perform simple and multi-level sorts
- Find records
- Filter data by selection
- Filter data by form
- Extract data from several tables
- Enter expressions into select queries
- Set up parameter queries
- Perform calculations on your data
- Check for the presence or absence of data.

08

reports

In this chapter you will learn:

- how to create reports
- how to create labels
- about grouping records in reports
- how to add page numbers and the date to reports
- about report calculations
- about formatting in reports

8.1 Introducing reports

Many of the terms and features used in Forms (see Chapter 6) also apply to reports. See section 6.1 for definitions of bound, unbound and calculated controls. The view options in Reports are also similar to those in Forms, with the exception of Print Preview.

You cannot edit the data in a report – if you want to edit something, go back to the table or query.

Report views

Report view: You can filter your data in report view, in a similar way to when working with queries.

Right-click on the column you want to filter and select the option required from the list.

Print Preview: This displays the report as it will look when printed. You can change the page setup and printing options from this view. If your report consists of several pages, you can use the navigation buttons at the bottom of the preview window to move through them.

Layout view: You can change the structure of your report and see the underlying data from your table or query at the same time. Being able to see your data while you adjust the structure of the report can be useful when deciding on the size that you want a control to be.

You will probably find that you can use Layout view to make most of the design changes you want on your report. To find out how to adjust controls in Layout view, see section 6.5.

Design view: This gives a more detailed view of the Report structure. You can't see the underlying data in this view, but there are a much wider range of controls available, e.g. images, lines, rectangles, etc.

- To change from one view to another, use the **View** button or the View tools at the bottom right of the window.

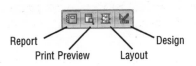

Report — Print Preview — Layout — Design

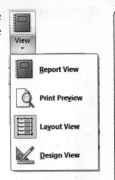

View
- Report View
- Print Preview
- Layout View
- Design View

8.2 The Report tool

You can quickly create a simple report from any of your tables or queries using the Report tool in the Reports group on the Create tab of the Ribbon. This feature is useful either just to give you an initial idea of how your data would look in a report, or as a starting point for further development of a report.

To create a report using the Report tool:

1 In the Navigation pane, select the table or query from which you want to create a report.

Or

- Open the table or query in Datasheet view.

2 Click **Report** in the **Reports** group on the **Create** tab.

- Your data will be presented in a basic report layout.

The report will be presented in Layout view. This view can be particularly useful if you want to adjust any field sizes on your report as the data is displayed in the field controls. You will notice several objects on your report that enhance the presentation of the data. e.g. headers and footers, and summary data.

- **Headers and footers areas:** The logo, report name, date and time are in the header, and page numbering is displayed in the footer in this example.

- **Summary data:** There is a calculated field under the *PublisherID* column, counting the number of publishers in the report.

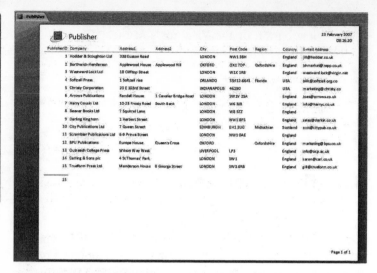

Report Layout tools

The Report Layout tools are displayed on the Format, Arrange and Page Setup tabs when you are in Layout view. Many of them are similar to those found in Form Layout view.

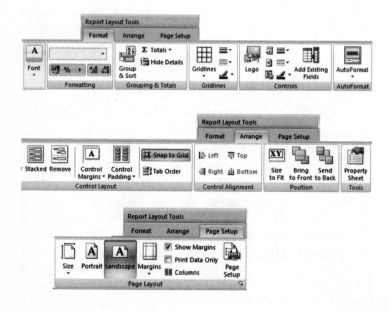

8.3 Blank report

If you prefer to start from a blank canvas, or wish to add data from more than one table or query to your report, you could use the Blank report option.

1 Click ▢ Blank Report in the **Reports** group on the **Create** tab.

♦ A blank report is displayed in Layout View.

2 Drag the fields required from the Field List displayed on the right, onto the form.

♦ Not all fields can be dragged into all areas – if you cannot get the layout you require you might need to use the Report Wizard or Design view.

♦ Click the ⊞ and ⊟ buttons to the left of the table names to expand and collapse the field lists.

3 Add controls, e.g. Logo, Title, Data and Time as required – (see section 6.5).

4 Save and close your report.

This report was created by dragging the fields required from the Book, Author and Category tables in to the Report area.

A Title and date were then added using controls in the Control group, and an AutoFormat was applied to finish it off!

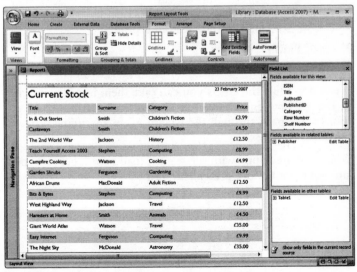

8.4 Labels

If any of your tables contain names and addresses, you may well need to prepare mailing labels from them from time to time. Labels can be set up in Access using the Labels Wizard.

To create labels:

1 In the Navigation pane, select the table or query from which you want to create your labels.

2 Click **Labels** in the **Reports** group on the **Create** tab.

• The **Label Wizard** dialog box appears, listing lots of different label specifications from various manufacturers. You can choose a label from those listed, or set up your own.

3 Select the label size required and click **Next**.

4 Set the font and font attributes and click **Next**.

5 Select the fields required for your label from the **Available fields** list and add them to the **Prototype label** layout.

6 Press [Enter] or add text and/or punctuation to get the layout required and click **Next**.

• If you add a field by mistake, select it in the **Prototype** and press [Delete].

7 Specify the sort order, e.g. *Company*.

8 At the chequered flag, edit the report name if necessary and choose **See labels as they will look printed**.

9 Click **Finish**.

• A Print Preview of the labels will appear on your screen.

If you don't like the labels you can take them into Layout view or Design view and change the font or font attributes, or you could work back through the wizard again specifying different criteria.

When you are happy with the results, load your label stationery into your printer and print them out.

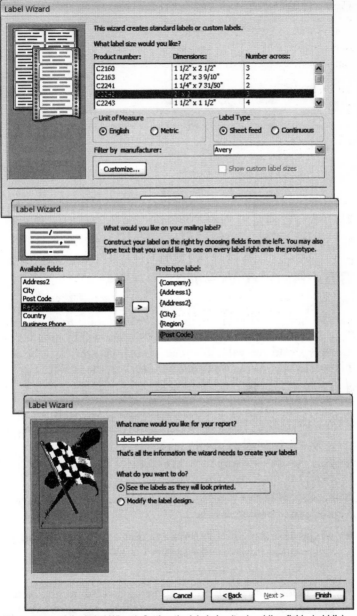

Three stages of the Label Wizard: Setting the label size (top), adding fields (middle) and saving the report (bottom).

```
Arrows Publications      Beaver Books Ltd      Borthwick-Henderson
Randall House            7 Squirrel Lane       Applewood House
1 Cavalier Bridge Road   LONDON                Applewood Hill
LONDON                   W8 5TZ                OXFORD
SW1V 2SA                                       Oxfordshire
                                               OX1 7DP



BPU Publications         Carling & Sons plc    Christy Corporation
Europa House             4 St Thomas' Park     20 E 103rd Street
Queen's Cross            LONDON                INDIANAPOLIS
OXFORD                   SW1                   46290
Oxfordshire



City Publications Ltd    Darling Kinghorn      Harry Cousin Ltd
7 Queen Street           2 Herbert Street      10-23 Frosty Road
EDINBURGH                LONDON                South Bank
Midlothian               NW1 8PS               LONDON
EH1 3UG                                        W6 8JB
```

Preview your labels before printing.

8.5 Report Wizard

The Report Wizard can help you produce some very sophisticated reports, very easily. In this report I am going to display the
data from the query *Value of Stock*. The data will be grouped by
Category, and the value of stock in each category will be displayed, as well as the total value of stock in the report.

1 Click **Report Wizard** in the **Reports** group.

2 Select the table or query that you want to create a report
from (you can select fields from different tables as long as
they are related).

3 Add the fields required to the **Selected Fields** list and click
Next.

4 Select a field (or fields) to group the data on – *Category* in
this case – and click **Next**.

5 At the next step, specify the sort order – the books are going
to be sorted into ascending order on *Title*.

6 Click **Summary Options...**

• The fields that calculations can be performed on will be displayed, together with the possible actions, e.g. sum, average,
minimum and maximum. We want to calculate the total value
of books in each category and in the whole report.

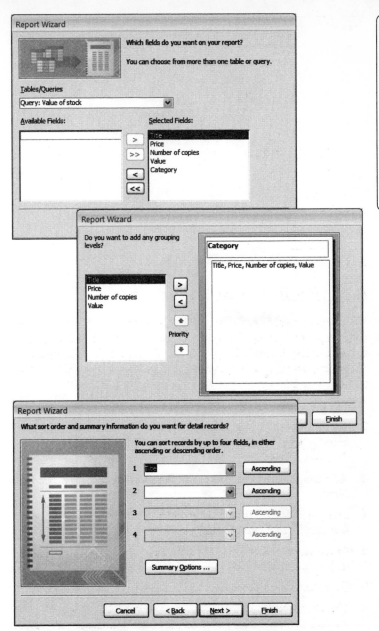

Selecting the tables/queries and adding fields (top), setting the grouping levels (middle) and setting the sort order and summary options (bottom).

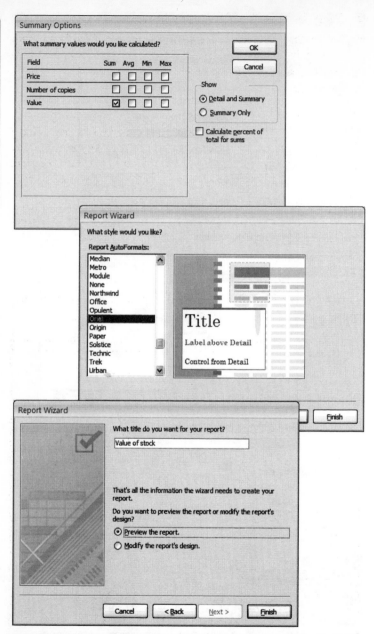

Setting up the calculated fields (top), choosing a style (middle) and giving the report a title at the finish (bottom).

7 Select the **Sum** checkbox in the **Value** row.

8 Set the **Show** option to **Detail and Summary** – the Detail will summarize the data after each group, the Summary will provide a grand total at the end.

9 Click **OK**.

10 Click **Next** at the sort options.

11 Choose a layout and orientation for your report (if you have lots of fields choose *Landscape*). Select the **Adjust** checkbox if necessary and Access will then fit your fields onto the page as best it can. Click **Next**.

12 Select an AutoFormat and click **Next**.

13 At the final step, edit the report name if necessary and select **Preview the Report**.

14 Click **Finish**!

Your report will be displayed.

Check out your report in Print Preview and see if there is anything that you want to change.

Value of stock

Category	Title	Price	Number of copies	Value
Adult Fiction				
	African Drums	£12.50	1	£12.50
Summary for 'Category' = Adult Fiction (1 detail record)				
Sum				£12.50
Animals				
	Hamsters at Home	£4.50	1	£4.50
Summary for 'Category' = Animals (1 detail record)				
Sum				£4.50
Astronomy				
	Changing Skies	£10.99	2	£21.98
	Crazy Comets	£17.50	1	£17.50
	The Night Sky	£35.00	2	£70.00
Summary for 'Category' = Astronomy (3 detail records)				
Sum				£109.48
Children's Fiction				
	Castaways	£4.50	2	£9.00
	In & Out Stories	£3.99	3	£11.97
	The Tortoise in the Corner	£6.50	2	£13.00
Summary for 'Category' = Children's Fiction (3 detail records)				
Sum				£33.97
Computing				
	Bits & Bytes	£9.99	2	£19.98
	Easy Internet	£9.99	2	£19.98
	Teach Yourself Access 2003	£8.99	2	£17.98
Summary for 'Category' = Computing (3 detail records)				
Sum				£57.94
Cooking				
	Bread and Biscuits	£12.50	2	£25.00
	Campfire Cooking	£4.99	1	£4.99
	Perfect Pizzas	£9.99	2	£19.98

Formatting on the calculated fields

Calculated fields do not automatically pick up a currency format. You can use the Currency option in the Formatting group on the Format tab to display the results as currency.

8.6 Report Design

You can design a report from scratch in Report Design, but most people use it to add the final touches. It is usually quicker to create your report using one of the other methods, and then use Report Design if you need to do something that can't be done easily elsewhere.

You might need to go into Report Design to add a page break in a specific place. If you wanted each book category to start on a new page the control can be added in Design view.

Report Design view is similar to Form Design view.

Take one of your reports into Design view.

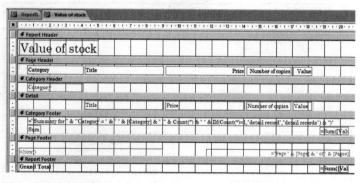

Report areas

The areas on this report are:

*   **Report Header** – anything in here is presented at the top of page 1 in the report.

*   **Page Header** – for information that is repeated at the top of each page.

*   **Category Header** – the Group Header for the Category field.

- **Detail** – lists information from the underlying table or query.

- **Category Footer** – the Group Footer for the Category field.

- **Page Footer** – for information that is repeated at the bottom of each page.

- **Report Footer** – anything in here is presented at the end of the report.

Report Design tools

The Report Design tools are displayed when you are in Design View. These are similar to those found in Form Design view, with additional ones specifically for reports, e.g. Group & Sort.

To add a page break under the Category group:

1 Select **Insert/Remove Page Break** 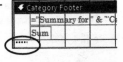 in the **Controls** group.

2 Click where you want the page break – at the bottom of the Category Footer. The page break control is displayed at the left edge of the report.

- If you look at the report in Print Preview, you will see that each Category starts on a new page.

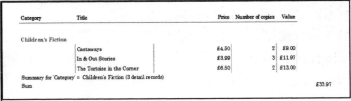

To delete the page break control:

1 Go into Design view.

2 Select the control – click on it.

3 Press **[Delete]**.

8.7 Printing your report

The **Page Layout** group is displayed on the Page Setup tab in the Report Layout Tools and when you are Print Previewing your report. This group gives you access to several options that affect the printout of reports. Paper size, orientation and margins can all be controlled from here.

If your data is going to be printed onto a pre-printed form, the **Print Data Only** option can be used.

The **Page Setup** button opens a dialog box that contains a few other options, giving you even more flexibility on specifying your requirements.

Once you have checked that you have the correct paper size, orientation, margins, etc. you are ready to print your report.

From Print Preview:

1 Click **Print**.

2 At the **Print** dialog box, specify the **Print Range**, **Number of copies**, etc.

3 Click **OK**.

From Report view:

1 Click the Microsoft Office button and choose **Print** from the menu.

2 Set your options in the **Print** dialog box.

3 Click **OK**.

Summary

In this chapter we have produced reports from the data held in your tables and queries. We have discussed:

* Using the Report tool to create a quick report
* Blank reports
* Creating labels using the Label Wizard
* Producing sophisticated reports using Report Wizard
* Adding grouping and summary calculations to reports
* Report Design view and inserting page breaks
* Printing reports.

09

pivottables and pivotcharts

In this chapter you will learn:

- how to display data in PivotTables
- about showing/hiding and filtering data
- some calculation options
- how to display and manipulate data in a PivotChart
- about multiple series

9.1 PivotTable view

Open the *Book* table in Datasheet view so that you can experiment with this feature.

* Click the drop-down arrow beside the **View** tool and choose **PivotTable View**.

An empty PivotTable is displayed, with a Field List showing which fields contain the source data that you have access to.

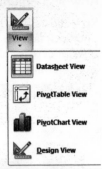

* Click **Field List** in the **Show/Hide** group to toggle the display of the field list.

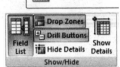

PivotTable tools

The PivotTable tools are displayed when you are in PivotTable view.

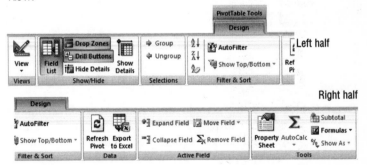

Areas

The PivotTable contains a number of 'drop' areas – areas into which you can drop the fields from your table.

Filter

A filter field is used to confine the view to a particular part of the available data. When an item is selected in a filter field, data is displayed and calculated only for that item. For example, if you add the Category Name field to the Drop Filter area, you can have the PivotTable view display and calculate data for the categories you select.

Row and column

Row and column fields are used to summarize and compare data. They display the unique items of data in a field either down rows or across columns. The cell at the intersection of each row and column summarizes the data for the item.

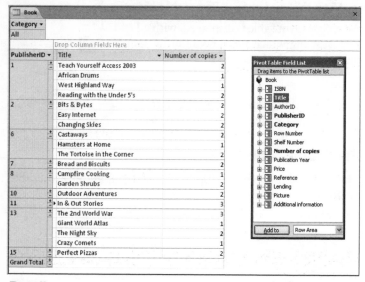

Detail

Detail fields display the actual data – that which is available to be summarized. They display all of the records from the source for these fields. Field names become column labels, with the detail records displayed in rows below them.

Add, remove and move fields

You must add the fields that you wish to display in the PivotTable to the row, column, filter and detail area (you don't need to add fields to all areas).

Field names in the List that are **bold** have already been added to the PivotTable, those that are not bold can be added as required.

To add a field:

- Drag and Drop the field into the appropriate area (depending on how you wish to filter and analyse your data).

Or

1 Select the field you wish to add to the PivotTable.

2 Choose the area that you want to add it to from the options (at bottom of the Field List).

3 Click **Add To**.

To remove a field:

1 Right-click on the field name in the PivotTable.

2 Left-click on **Remove**.

Or

1 Click anywhere within the field.

2 Click **Remove Field** in the **Active Field** group.

Add the following fields to the areas suggested:

Filter	Category Name and Publisher ID
Row	Title
Column	Number of copies
Detail	Price

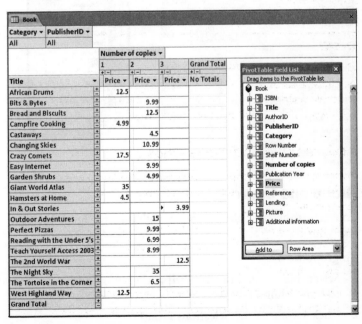

To move a field:

1 Click on the field name at the top of the
column or to the left of a row.

2 Click **Move Field** in the **Active Field**
group.

3 Select a new location from the list.

Or

* Drag and drop the field from one area to another. Watch the
icon that appears at the pointer as you drag and drop – it lets
you know which area you are over.

Your data will 'pivot' when you move fields – hence the name!

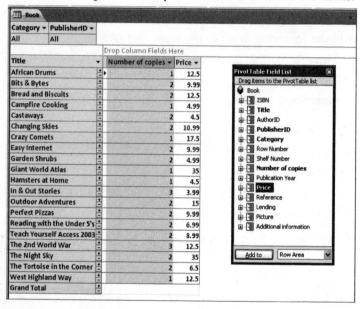

Group and Ungroup

You can group the fields in your PivotTable if it helps you analyse your data.

To group fields:

1 Select them – hold down [Ctrl] and click on each
row or column label.

2 Click **Group** in the **Selections** group.

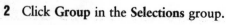

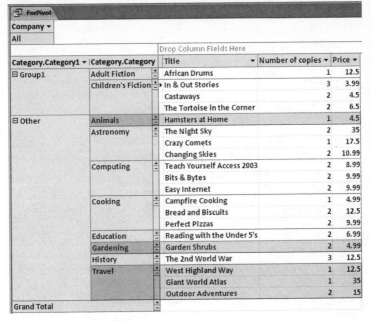

Rename groups

To give the groups meaningful names, you can rename them in
their Property Sheet.

1 Click on the group name, e.g. *Group1*.

2 Click **Property Sheet** in the **Tools** group.

3 Edit the caption
as required.

4 Close the dialog
box.

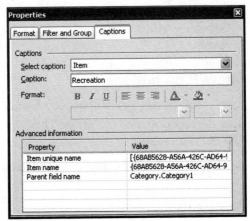

Category.Category1 ▾	Category.Category	Title ▾	Number of copies ▾	Price ▾
⊟ Fiction	Adult Fiction ±	African Drums	1	12.5
	Children's Fiction ±	In & Out Stories	3	3.99
		Castaways	2	4.5
		The Tortoise in the Corner	2	6.5
⊟ Science	Astronomy ±	The Night Sky	2	35
		Crazy Comets	1	17.5
		Changing Skies	2	10.99
	Computing ±	Teach Yourself Access 2003	2	8.99
		Bits & Bytes	2	9.99
		Easy Internet	2	9.99
⊟ Recreation	Animals ±	Hamsters at Home	1	4.5
	Cooking ±	Campfire Cooking	1	4.99
		Bread and Biscuits	2	12.5
		Perfect Pizzas	2	9.99
	Gardening ±	Garden Shrubs	2	4.99
⊟ General Education	Education ±	Reading with the Under 5's	2	6.99
	History ±	The 2nd World War	3	12.5
	Travel ±	West Highland Way	1	12.5
		Giant World Atlas	1	35
		▸ Outdoor Adventures	2	15

To expand and collapse a group:

1 Select the group – click on its name.

2 Click **Expand** or **Collapse** in the **Active Field** group.

Or

• Click the ⊞ or ⊟ to the left of the group name.

To ungroup:

• Select the group name and click **Ungroup** in the **Selections** group.

Show/Hide buttons

If you look closely you will notice plus and minus signs at the Row ⊞ and Column ⊞⊟ areas. These are used to show and hide the information in that row or column.

• Click ⊞ to show the data or ⊟ to hide it.

Show/Hide Details

You can also use the **Show/Hide Details** button to toggle the display of your data.

1 Select the Filter, Row, Column or Data field name.

2 Click **Show/Hide Details** button in the **Show/Hide** group.

♦ You can show/hide the information in individual rows and columns if you select the row or column then click the **Show Details** or **Hide Details** button.

Filter

Use the Filter fields to display specific sets of data.

1 Click the arrow by the field you wish to filter on, e.g. *Number of copies*.

2 Deselect the **All** checkbox.

3 Select the number you wish to display.

4 Click **OK**.

AutoFilter

Click **AutoFilter** in the **Filter & Sort** group to toggle between showing all the items in a PivotTable and those in a filtered list.

Show Top/Bottom items

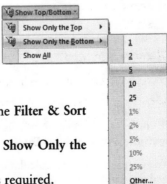

You can choose to show the top or bottom items in your rows or columns.

1 Click on the row heading or column heading area.

2 Click **Show Top/Bottom** in the **Filter & Sort** group.

3 Select **Show Only the Top** or **Show Only the Bottom**.

4 Click on the number of items required.

AutoCalc and Subtotal

Calculations can be performed on the data identified in the rows and columns.

To toggle the display of a subtotal row or column:

1 Select the row or column field name.

2 Click **Subtotal** in the **Tools** group.

To perform an automatic calculation:

1 Select the row or column field name.

2 Click **AutoCalc** in the **Tools** group.

3 Select the type of calculation required from the list.

When you have performed calculations on your data, an entry appears under **Totals** in the Field List.

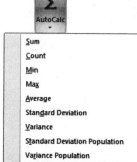

Σ
AutoCalc

Sum
Count
Min
Max
Average
Standard Deviation
Variance
Standard Deviation Population
Variance Population

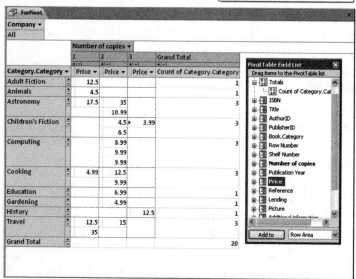

Category.Category ▾	Number of copies ▾			Grand Total	
	1	2	3		
	Price ▾	Price ▾	Price ▾	Count of Category.Category	
Adult Fiction	12.5				1
Animals	4.5				1
Astronomy	17.5	35			3
		10.99			
Children's Fiction		4.5 ▸	3.99		3
		6.5			
Computing		8.99			3
		9.99			
		9.99			
Cooking	4.99	12.5			3
		9.99			
Education		6.99			1
Gardening		4.99			1
History			12.5		1
Travel	12.5	15			3
	35				
Grand Total					20

PivotTable Field List

Drag items to the PivotTable list

⊞ Totals
 └ Count of Category.Cat
⊞ ISBN
⊞ Title
⊞ AuthorID
⊞ PublisherID
⊞ Book.Category
⊞ Row Number
⊞ Shelf Number
⊞ **Number of copies**
⊞ Publication Year
⊞ **Price**
⊞ Reference
⊞ Lending
⊞ Picture
⊞ Additional information

Add to   Row Area

If you perform several calculations on your data, there will be multiple entries under **Totals**.

You can remove your calculations from the PivotTable in the normal way (right-click on the column heading, then click on **Remove**).

The calculation is not deleted – it remains in the Field List and can be added to the PivotTable again (double-click on it).

- To delete a calculation, right-click on it in the Field List and click **Delete**.

ForPivot					
Company ▾					
All					
		Drop Column Fields Here			
Category.Category1 ▾	Category.Category	Title ▾		Number of copies ▾	Price ▾
⊟ Group1	Adult Fiction	African Drums		1	12.5
	Children's Fiction	▶ In & Out Stories		3	3.99
		Castaways		2	4.5
		The Tortoise in the Corner		2	6.5
⊟ Other	Animals	Hamsters at Home		1	4.5
	Astronomy	The Night Sky		2	35
		Crazy Comets		1	17.5
		Changing Skies		2	10.99
	Computing	Teach Yourself Access 2003		2	8.99
		Bits & Bytes		2	9.99
		Easy Internet		2	9.99
	Cooking	Campfire Cooking		1	4.99
		Bread and Biscuits		2	12.5
		Perfect Pizzas		2	9.99
	Education	Reading with the Under 5's		2	6.99
	Gardening	Garden Shrubs		2	4.99
	History	The 2nd World War		3	12.5
	Travel	West Highland Way		1	12.5
		Giant World Atlas		1	35
		Outdoor Adventures		2	15
Grand Total					

9.2 PivotCharts

A PivotChart gives a graphical representation of your data.

To go into PivotChart view:

- Click the arrow under the **View** button and choose **PivotChart View**.

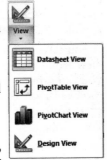

View
▾

Datasheet View

PivotTable View

PivotChart View

Design View

If you go into PivotChart from a PivotTable, the data in the PivotTable is automatically presented in the PivotChart.

You can move fields from one area of the PivotChart to another and filter your fields in the same way as you do in a PivotTable.

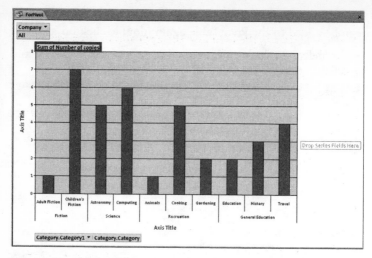

PivotChart tools

The PivotChart tools are displayed when you are in PivotChart view.

If you have not created a PivotTable, and go into PivotChart view from your datasheet, an empty chart is displayed, so that you can arrange your chart as required by dragging fields from the Field List. You can add, remove and move the fields to display your data using the same techniques as you do in a PivotTable.

Add, remove and move fields

You must add the fields that you wish to display in the PivotChart to the filter, category, series and data areas (you don't need to add fields to all areas).

To add a field:

- Drag and drop the field into the appropriate area (depending on how you wish to filter and analyse your data).

Or

1 Select the field you wish to add to the PivotChart.

2 Choose the area that you want to add it to from the options (at bottom of Field List).

3 Click **Add To.**

To remove a field:

1 Click on the field in the PivotChart.

2 Press [Delete].

To move a field:

- Drag and Drop the fields from one area to another to move them and 'pivot' the data.

Add the following fields to the areas suggested:

Filter	Company
Series	Category
Data	Number of copies

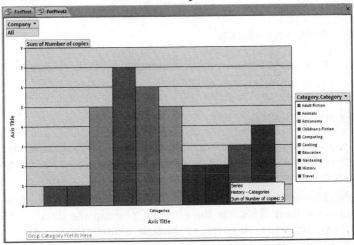

- Click **Legend** in the **Show/Hide** group to display the legend.

- Click the drop-down arrows beside the filter and legend fields to control the amount of data displayed.

Edit the chart type

1 Click on the Chartspace – the area surrounding your chart,
   or on its Plot area.

2 Click **Change Chart Type** in the **Type** group to display the **Properties** dialog box.

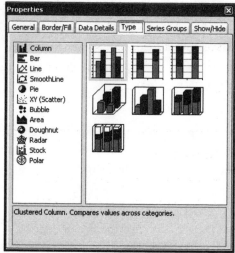

3 Select the **Type**
   tab.

4 Pick a type from
   the list of charts
   down the left.

5 Choose a chart
   from the options
   on the right.

6 Close the **Proper-
   ties** dialog box.

By row/By column

Click [Switch Row/Column] in the **Active field** group to change from
a by-row representation of the data to a by-column one.

Multiple series

You can plot more than one series of data on your chart. In this
example both *Publication Year* and *Category Name* have been
added to the Category fields area.

Publication Year is at the **outer** level, and *Category Name* is at
an **inner** level. This has the effect of plotting the data in the
outer level, and then moves to the right plotting the inner levels
within the higher level.

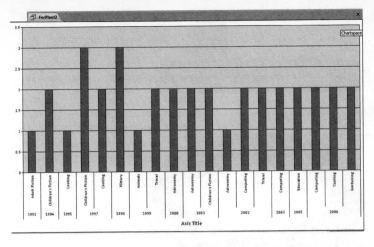

Summary

In this chapter we have discussed:

- Displaying data in a PivotTable
- Adding, removing and moving fields in a PivotTable
- The Show and Hide options
- Filtering the data
- Automatic calculations
- Displaying data in a PivotChart
- Adding, removing and moving fields in a PivotChart
- The Legend display
- Selecting a different Chart Type
- Arranging data by row and by column
- Multiple series.

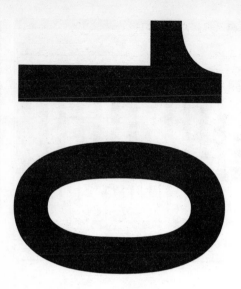

10

templates

In this chapter you will learn:

- how to create a database from a template
- about the Contacts template
- how to use table templates

10.1 Database templates

Rather than create a database from scratch as we have in the Library project, you may find that you can create a database quickly from one of the many database templates that are provided. You will find some templates installed locally on your computer; others can be located online.

To create a database using a template:

1 Select **Local Templates** in the **Template Categories** on the **Getting Started with Microsoft Office Access** screen.

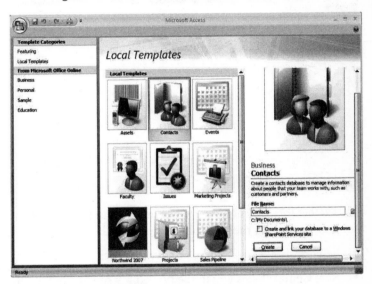

2 Choose a template from those displayed.

3 Check/edit the filename and location as necessary.

4 Click **Create**.

A new database will be created, with tables, forms, queries and reports, depending on which template you chose.

You will also find many more templates online – just choose one of the online categories at step 1 above.

10.2 Exploring your database

Take some time to explore the database. With one created from the Contacts template, the database opens at the Contact List form, ready for data entry and edit operations.

All you have to do is type in your list!

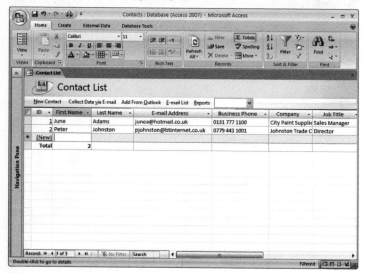

Notice the *Total* calculation control underneath the First Name column, displaying the total number of records entered.

In the Form header area there are five options:

- **New Contact** takes you to the first empty row ready for data entry.

- **Collect Data via E-mail** allows you to send out forms. The address of the recipients and the data they return can be stored in the database automatically or manually, if required.

- **Add from Outlook** opens a dialog box where you can select contacts from Outlook and add them to your database.

- **E-mail list** lets you send the list as an e-mail attachment.

- **Reports** displays a list of reports that are set up in your database. Just select one to open it.

When the insertion point is in the *First Name* or *Last Name* field, there is a message in the Status bar – double-click to go to details. This opens the Contact Details form so you can add or edit the information on your contact.

In the Contact Details form, the data is Filtered (see Status bar).

• The **Go to** field in the Form header area is a drop-down list that allows you to select other contacts.

• The **E-mail** option displays an e-mail dialog box so you can send an e-mail directly from your database.

• **Create Outlook Contact** adds the contact to your Outlook Contacts list.

• **Save and New** saves the changes and presents a new blank form for you to complete.

• **Close** returns you to the Contact List form.

10.3 Navigation pane

If you look at the Navigation pane you will see the objects that have been used in setting up this database. Look again and you will see that the objects are really shortcuts to other objects.

There are shortcuts to:

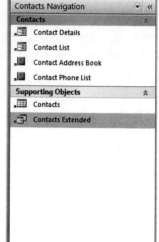

- Two forms – *Contact Details* and *Contact List*.

- Two reports – *Contact Address Book* and *Contact Phone List*.

- One Table – *Contacts*.

- One Query – *Contacts Extended*.

You should open the objects in Design view so that you can check out how they have been set up.

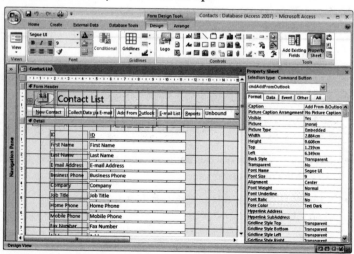

For example, if you take the Contact Details form into Design view you will notice that most of the buttons in the Form Header area are Command Buttons. The Report list is a combo box.

You may not understand everything about how the database has been constructed but you should have a fair idea about quite a bit of what you find. Exploring the structures of the databases created by templates is a good way to see how some of the features can be used, and also introduce some new ones that you can investigate.

10.4 Table templates

You will also find a selection of table templates to choose from. You can create a table in any database using a table template.

To create a table from a table template:

1 Display the **Create** tab on the Ribbon.

2 Click **Table Templates** in the **Table** group.

3 Select a template from the list.

A new table is created within the open database.

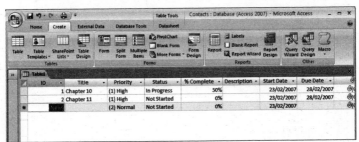

You can adjust the table structure, save your table and enter and edit data as you would with any other table.

Summary

This chapter introduced some of the templates that are provided in Access. We have discussed:

- Creating a database from a template
- Exploring the database
- The Navigation pane for the database
- Creating tables from templates.

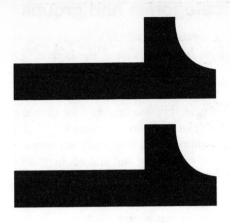

11

categories and groups

In this chapter you will learn:

- how to create a custom category
- how to add groups to a category
- how to add objects to a group
- how to maintain your groups

11.1 Objects, categories and groups

In the previous chapter we created a database using a template. When you create a database from a template, the objects that appear in the Navigation pane are really shortcuts to the original objects.

Creating shortcuts to objects in this way makes your database more secure – it can prevent users from accidentally deleting objects (imagine deleting a table with all your customer contacts in it, or even your Christmas card name and address list!).

In previous versions of Access, switchboards were used to keep users at a distance from the primary objects. In Access 2007 the Navigation pane can be used for this purpose.

To create shortcuts to your objects you need to:

◆ Create a custom category – you can have a maximum of 10 custom categories within a database.

◆ Create groups within your category – you can have as many groups as you need within a category.

◆ Add objects to the custom groups.

◆ Hide the original objects.

To create a custom category:

1 Right-click on the Navigation pane menu bar.

2 Choose **Navigation Options...**

3 At the **Navigation Options** dialog box, click **Add Item** under the **Categories** column (left side).

4 Give your custom category a name – use one that reflects its contents, or will make sense to those who use it.

5 Press **[Enter]**.

◆ Access automatically creates a group within your new category called *Unassigned Objects*.

To create groups within the category:

1 Select a category in the **Categories** list.

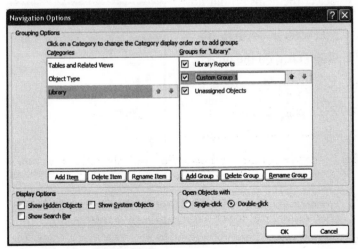

2 Click **Add Group** under the **Groups** list.

3 Give your group a name and press [**Enter**].

4 Repeat steps 2–3 until you have all your groups set up.

5 Click **OK** to close the **Navigation Options** dialog box.

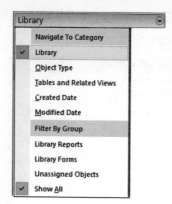

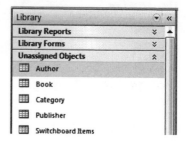

Display your category in the Navigation pane – select it from the menu. Your category will appear at the top of the pane, and the groups will be listed below it.

11.2 Adding objects to groups

The next step is to copy the objects that you want in your groups from the Unassigned Objects group.

1 Select the items – hold down [Ctrl] and click on each item you want in any one group.

2 Right click on the objects.

3 Click on **Add to group...**, and then on the group name, e.g. *Library Forms*.

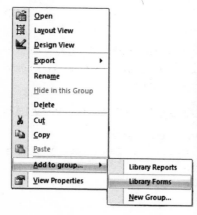

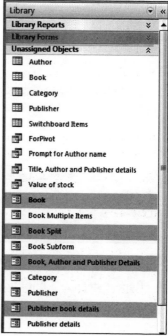

- Alternatively, drag and drop the item(s) onto the group.

When you add objects to a group a shortcut is created to the object. The object – table, query, form or report – remains in its original location.

If a shortcut is deleted or moved, the original object is not affected.

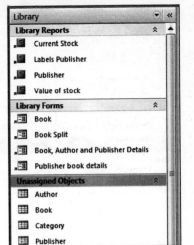

11.3 Hiding groups and objects

To further protect your objects from users or accidental errors you can hide them.

There are two ways to hide objects in Access.

You can:

- Hide an object from the parent group and category using commands in the Navigation pane.

Or

- Choose a property for each object to hide it from all groups and categories in the database.

You can also make hidden objects completely invisible, or you can choose to display them dimmed – so that they can be seen in the Navigation pane, but are unavailable.

The option to show hidden objects or not is controlled from the Navigation Options dialog box.

You could hide the Unassigned Objects group once you have your custom groups populated.

To hide a group:

1 Right-click on its title bar.

2 Choose **Hide**.

To unhide a group:

1 Open the **Navigation Options** dialog box (right-click on the Navigation pane menu bar and choose **Navigation Options...**)

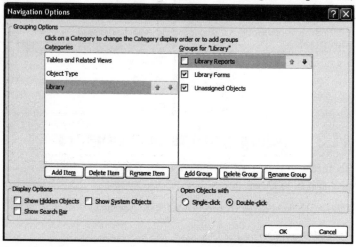

2 Select the group's Category from the list on the left.

3 On the right, select the checkbox next to the group you want to unhide.

4 Click **OK**.

To hide an object in its parent group:

1 Right-click on the object.

2 Choose **Hide in this Group** from the list of options.

To hide an object from all groups and categories:

1 Right-click on the object.

2 Choose **View Properties**.

The name of the object appears in the title bar.

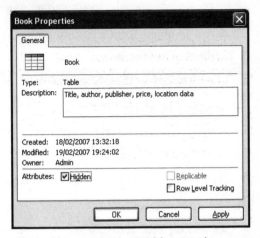

3 In the **Properties** dialog box, select the **Hidden** attribute.

4 Click **OK**.

To restore hidden objects:

1 Display the **Navigation Options** dialog box.

2 Select the **Show Hidden Objects** checkbox and click **OK**.

♦ Your hidden objects should appear dimmed in the Navigation panel.

To remove the hidden property:

♦ If you hid the object from its parent group: right-click on it and then click **Unhide** in this Group.

♦ If you hid the object from all groups and categories: display the **Properties** dialog box for the object (right-click on it and choose **View Properties**) and deselect the **Hidden** attribute.

11.4 Custom group maintenance

Over time, you may need to update your custom groups, e.g. by adding new object shortcuts, deleting ones you no longer need, or by renaming shortcuts to something more appropriate.

To delete an object from a custom group:

1 Right-click on the item.

2 Click **Remove** in the context menu.

To rename a shortcut:

1 Right-click on the item.

2 Click **Rename Shortcut**.

3 Type in the new name and press [**Enter**].

To add new objects:

• See section 11.2 above.

By creating custom groups and hiding the Unassigned group, our Library database would look something like this.

The main objects are safely tucked away from your users making serious errors (accidental deletion of tables or form, query and report designs) more difficult.

Summary

In this chapter we have discussed:

- Creating custom categories and groups
- Adding objects to the groups
- Hiding and showing groups and objects
- Managing your custom groups.

12

macros

In this chapter you will learn:

- about creating and running macros
- how to assign a macro to a control button

12.1 Introducing macros

Macros are used to automate the execution of a specific sequence of actions. They can either be embedded within an object, e.g. a form or report, or they can be created as *macro objects* (these are sometimes called standalone macros). Embedded macros are part of the object that they are created in, macro objects are listed in the Navigation panel with the other objects in your database.

In Chapter 6 (section 6.14), we added a Command button to a form. This is an example of an embedded macro. When the command button is clicked, the Print a Form action is carried out. Macros can be used for similar and more sophisticated routines.

In our Library database we can open the objects we are working on from the Navigation pane, and then move from one open object to the next using the object tabs.

You can use macros for many things, including:

◆ Open a table, form, query or report in any available view.

◆ Close an open table, form, query or report.

◆ Open a report in Print Preview.

◆ Send a report to the printer.

This chapter gives you an introduction to macros in Access. You will find further information in the Help system.

12.2 Recording a macro object

Let's say we had decided that we wanted to be able to open our *Publisher detail* form and our *Books grouped by category* report from within the *Book, Author and Publisher* form.

The first thing we need to do is record two macros:

◆ one containing the instructions to open the *Publisher detail* form in Form view.

◆ one containing the instructions to open the *Books grouped by category* report in Print Preview.

The Macro Builder is used to create macros.

To create a macro:

1 Display the **Create** tab in the Ribbon.

2 Click **Macro,** and then **Macro** in the **Other** group.

♦ The Macro Builder window is displayed.

3 Select an action from the options in the **Action** column – **OpenForm** in this case.

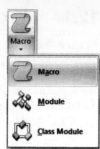

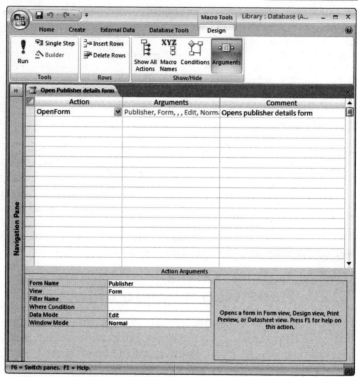

4 Enter a description of what the action will achieve in the **Comment** column. This is optional – it simply says what will happen – you can leave the column blank if you wish.

5 Choose the form in the **Form Name** field in the lower pane.

6 Specify the view that you want the form displayed in.

7 Set the **Data Mode** to **Edit**.

8 Save your macro. Give it a name that describes what it does to make it easier to remember.

9 Close your macro.

Create another macro, this time to open one of your reports.

1 Click **Macro,** and then **Macro** in the **Other** group on the **Create** tab.

2 Select an action from the **Action** column – **OpenReport** in this example.

3 Enter a description in the **Comment** column if you wish.

4 Choose the report in the **Report Name** field in the lower pane.

5 Specify the view that you want the report to be displayed in – Report is the most likely.

6 Save your macro and close it.

The macros will be listed in the Navigation pane.

12.3 Testing the macros

To test your macros just double-click on them.

The actions recorded in the macro will be executed – the form and report should be opened.

If a macro doesn't do as you expected, for example it might open the wrong form or report, take it into Design view and amend your settings.

1 Right-click on the macro in the Navigation pane.

2 Click on **Design View.**

12.4 Adding the macro to a form

We want to be able to execute the macros that we have recorded from the Books form, so we can go directly from the Books form to the Publisher form and also to the chosen report. Macros created in this way can be added to more than one object in your database if you wish.

To add your macros to the form:

1 Display the form in Design view.

2 Adjust the layout if necessary, to make room for the macros – I have opted to put them in the Form Footer area.

3 Drag the macros from the Navigation pane and drop them into your form.

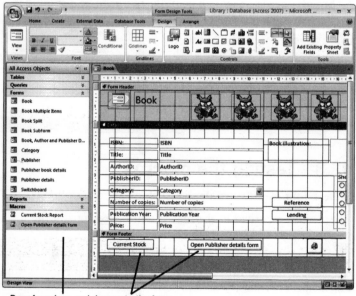

Drag from here and drop onto the form

4 Reposition and resize the macro command buttons as necessary.

5 Save your form.

Take your form into Form view and test out the buttons.

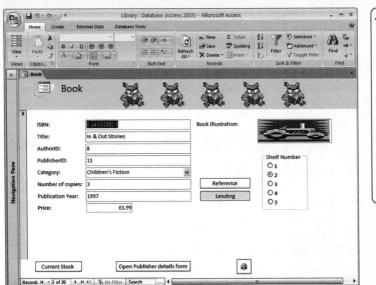

12.5 Embedded macros

Embedded macros are created within the object that you want to execute them from. They do not appear in the Navigation pane.

To create an embedded macro:

1 In Design view, open the object, e.g. a form or report, in which you want to create the macro.

2 Display the Property Sheet.

3 Select the control or section that you want to embed the macro in.

4 In the **Property Sheet** select the **Event** tab.

5 Click the event property that you want to run the macro, and click the Build button to the right of it.

6 Choose **Macro Builder** at the **Choose Builder** dialog box and click **OK**.

In this example:

- A Label has been added to the Report Header area.
- The Property Sheet has the **On Click** event chosen.
- The macro **Action** is set to *Close* and the **Arguments** have been set to the *Report*, *Current Stock* and *Prompt to Save*.

Label   On Click event added

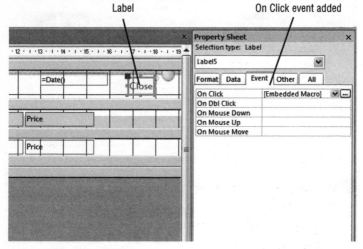

Macro action defined

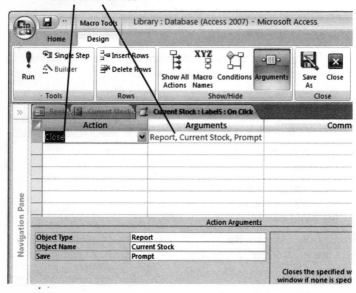

Macro tested

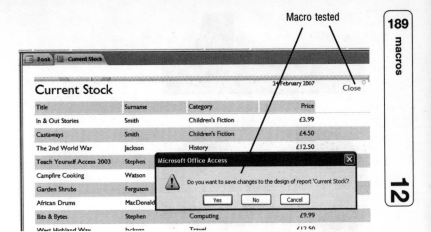

Summary

This chapter has introduced you to macros. We have discussed:

- Creating a macro object
- The Macro Builder
- Adding macros to forms and reports
- Creating embedded macros.

13

security and confidentiality

In this chapter you will learn:

- about backups
- how to protect data with passwords
- about hiding objects to protect them

13.1 Backups

Back up your data!!

If you have spent hours/days/weeks building up your database, you don't want to lose the results of your labours if your disk gets damaged or the file corrupted.

The simple solution has nothing to do with Access – just basic common sense! *Always* keep an up-to-date backup of your database. You could:

*   Copy the file onto CD or a pen drive
*   Use Windows Backup
*   Compress a large file with WinZip and then copy it.

It may take a few minutes to make a copy of your data, but it will have taken a lot longer for you to create your database, enter data, create queries, forms and reports, etc.

How often you take backups depends on how often your database changes. If you input and edit data each day, take a new backup each day. If your database doesn't change much, take a new backup when it does. Some companies backup their data several times a day, some may do it every few days – it depends how quickly it becomes out of date.

Store the backup copies somewhere safe – ideally away from your computer. If your computer gets stolen, the data on the hard drive goes with it. If your office gets damaged by flood or fire, the hard drive may be useless. If you have your backup CD stored in another room or building it should escape any problem your main computer suffers from – then you can copy the data onto another machine and be up and running again in no time!

Don't think it can't happen to you. *Back up your data!!*

13.2 Database password

You can restrict access to a database by protecting it with a password. This ensures that only those who know the password can open and edit the database. You must open a database for **Exclusive Use** when you wish to set or unset a password.

To open database for exclusive use:

1 Display the **Open** dialog box.

2 Select the database to open.

3 Click the drop-down arrow beside **Open**.

4 Choose **Open Exclusive**.

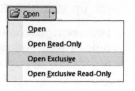

To set a password:

1 Open the database for exclusive use.

2 Display the **Database Tools** tab on the Ribbon.

3 Click **Encrypt with Password** in the **Database Tools** group.

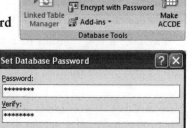

4 Enter the password in the **Password** field.

5 Type it again in the **Verify** field.

6 Click **OK**.

The next time you open your database you will be prompted for the password.

To remove the password from your database:

1 Open the database.

2 Click **Decrypt Database** in the **Database Tools** group.

3 Enter the password at the prompt.

4 Click **OK**.

Confidentiality of personal data

The data held in databases is often personal data – it identifies a person. You are legally required (Data Protection Act, 1998) to protect the confidentiality of personal data, and restricting access to your databases in this way can help ensure that confidentiality is maintained.

13.3 Hidden objects

One of the biggest threats to the security of data is the person using the computer. Lack of training and experience, or just accidental operator error, can have a devastating effect on data. It is a lot easier to delete tables, queries, forms and reports than it is to create them (just select them in the Navigation pane and press [Delete]).

You certainly don't want your tables to be accidentally deleted – they may contain data that would take days, weeks or even months to re-create (unless, or course, you have a backup – see section 13.1).

To help protect your data against possible operator error, you could hide any objects in your database (particularly the tables) that your users don't need to see, so that only those required (queries, forms, reports) are displayed.

It is particularly important to protect your tables, as this is where your data is actually stored.

See Chapter 11 for information on hiding objects.

Summary

In this chapter we have discussed:

* The importance of backups
* Restricting database access using passwords
* The option to hide database objects.

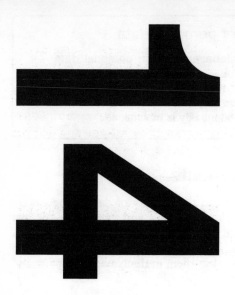

14

sharing data

In this chapter you will learn:

- about sending data via e-mail
- how to import data from another database
- how to export data to Excel

14.1 E-mail

If you are e-mailing your database there are several options that you could consider. You could send the whole database as an attached file. There are at least a couple of potential problems with this – one is security and the other is that some e-mail systems won't accept database attachments, as they are a potential virus risk. You can however e-mail the information that you have in individual tables or queries as an attachment.

To e-mail your data as an attachment:

1 Select the object in the Navigation pane.

2 Click the Microsoft Office button and choose **E-mail** from the menu.

3 Select the output format for your data and click **OK**.

4 Complete your message and send.

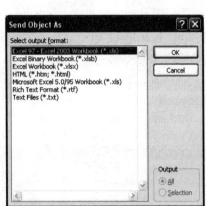

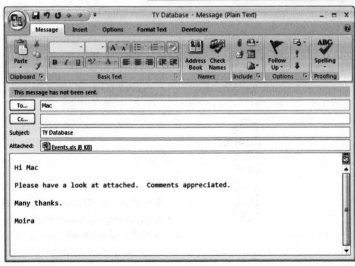

14.2 Importing data

There may be times when you need data that is held elsewhere – perhaps in another Access database, or an Excel file – in the database that you are working on.

Data that is held outside your database can be imported into the current database, or you can create a link to the data.

The Import options are on the External Data tab. When you select an Import option you will be prompted for the information required – just respond to the prompts to tell Access where to find the data and how you want it imported.

To import from another Access database:

1 Click **Access** in the **Import** group.

2 Specify the data source at the **Get External Data** dialog box – click **Browse** to locate the file if necessary.

Get External Data - Access Database   ? ×

Select the source and destination of the data

Specify the source of the data.

File name: C:\Documents and Settings\All Users\Documents\Moira\Books\2007 Access\Library.accdb   Browse...

Specify how and where you want to store the data in the current database.

○ **Import tables, queries, forms, reports, macros, and modules into the current database.**
If the specified object does not exist, Access will create it. If the specified object already exists, Access will append a number to the name of the imported object. Changes made to source objects (including data in tables) will not be reflected in the current database.

◉ **Link to the data source by creating a linked table.**
Access will create a table that will maintain a link to the source data. Changes made to the data in Access will be reflected in the source and vice versa. NOTE: If the source database requires a password, the password will be stored with the linked table.

OK   Cancel

3 Specify how your want the data imported – the usual choices are **Import** (effectively copies the data in) or **Link** (leaves the data in the original file, but you create a link to it).

4 Click **OK**.

5 Depending on the options chosen, you may be prompted for more information. With an Access database you will be asked to identify the tables required.

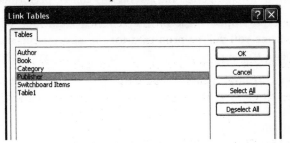

6 Select the tables and click **OK**.

• The table, or the link to it, will be displayed in the Navigation pane. Double-click on it to view the data.

If you link to a data source that changes regularly you might need to update your link to ensure that you are seeing the current data.

To refresh the data:

1 Right-click on the link.

2 Click **Linked Table Manager.**

3 Select the links you want updated in the dialog box.

4 Click **OK**.

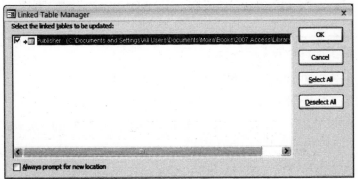

14.3 Exporting data

There may be times when you need to export your data in another format – perhaps so colleagues who don't have Access can use it, or so that additional operations can be performed on it.

The Export options are on the External Data tab. When you select one you will be prompted for the information required – respond to the prompts to tell Access how to export the data.

To export to an Excel spreadsheet:

1 Click **Excel** in the **Export** group.

2 Verify/edit the **File name** as required.

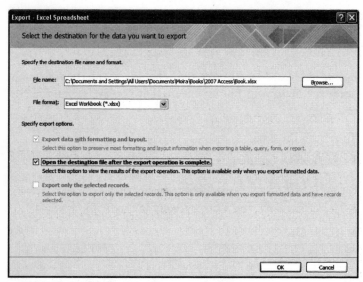

3 Choose the **File format**.

4 Set any other export options as necessary.

5 Click **OK**.

6 If the export action is something that you do regularly, you could save the export steps.

7 Click **OK**.

Your exported data can then be viewed and manipulated in Excel. If you saved your export information you can perform the same operation again from the Manage Data Tasks dialog box.

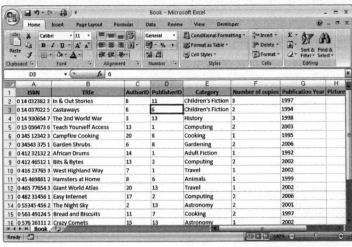

1   Click **Saved Exports** in the Export group.

2   Select an Export format.

3   Click **Run**.

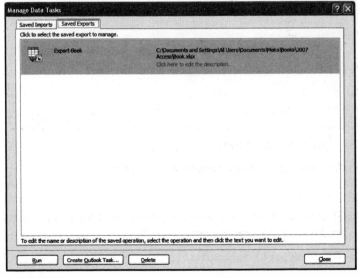

Summary

In this chapter we have discussed:

* Distributing data from your database via e-mail
* Importing data from other sources
* Exporting your Access data.

appendix: data tables

Sample data for the Library database tables

- author
- publisher
- book
- category

Author table data

AuthorID	Surname	Firstname	Date of Birth	Date of Death
1	Peterson	Brian		
2	McDonald	Alastair	12/01/36	
3	Jackson	Marion	24/06/55	
4	Adamson	Pauline		
5	Duncan	Wilma	04/07/38	
6	Ferguson	John	03/04/03	05/10/88
7	Jackson	Allan	10/12/40	02/10/93
8	Smith	Dick		
9	Schmit	Hans	12/12/52	
10	Camembert	Marion		
11	Meunier	Luc		
12	Allan	Isabelle	10/05/65	
13	Stephen	Moira		
14	MacDonald	Donald	12/12/20	01/03/78
15	Williams	Peter	10/10/30	
16	Borthwick	Anne		
17	Ferguson	Alan	04/12/45	
18	Wilson	Peter	12/01/30	
19	Smith	Ann		
20	Watson	George	22/10/45	

Nationality	Speciality	Notes
English	Romantic Fiction	Best seller "Hollywood Days"
Scottish	Poetry	
English	Travel	
Australian	Children's Fiction	
American	Travel	
Irish	Gardening	
Scottish	Travel	
Canadian	Children's Fiction	Best seller "The Mountie"
German	Computing	PC applications
French	Gardening	Best seller "Flowering Shrubs"
French	Cooking	
Scottish	Travel	
Scottish	Computing	PC applications
Scottish	Travel	
Irish	Science	School textbooks – mainly physics
Welsh	Astronomy	TV personality
English	Computing	Mainly Computer Science
Canadian	Children's Fiction	Famous for "Worst Wizard" books
American	Computing	PC applications
Austrian	Travel	Writer of TV books

Publisher table data

PublisherID	PublisherName	Address1	Address2	City	PostCode
1	Hodder & Stoughton Ltd	338 Euston Road		LONDON	NW1 3BH
2	Borthwick-Henderson	Applewood House	Applewood Hill	OXFORD	OX1 7DP
3	Westward Lock Ltd	18 Clifftop Street		LONDON	W1X 1RB
4	Softcell Press	One Softcell Rise		ORLANDO	33412-6641
5	Christy Corporation	20 E 103rd Street		INDIANAPOLIS	46290
6	Arrows Publications	Randall House	1 Cavalier Bridge Rd	LONDON	SW1V 2SA
7	Harry Cousin Ltd	10–23 Frosty Road	South Bank	LONDON	W6 8JB
8	Beaver Books Ltd	7 Squirrel Lane		LONDON	W8 5TZ
9	Darling Kinghorn Ltd	2 Herbert Street		LONDON	WC2E 8PS
10	City Publications Ltd	7 Queen Street		EDINBURGH	EH1 3UG
11	Scrambler Publications Ltd	6–9 Prince Street		LONDON	NW1 0AE
12	BPU Publications	Europa House	Queen's Cross	OXFORD	
13	Outreach College Press	Wilson Way West		LIVERPOOL	LP3
14	Carling & Sons plc	4 St Thomas' Park		LONDON	SW1
15	Trueform Press Ltd	Manderson House	8 George Street	LONDON	SW3 6RB

Publisher table data (cont.)

County	Country	Phone Number	Fax Number	E-mail Address	Website
	England	020 7738 6060	020 7738 9926	jill@hodder.co.uk	Hodder & Stoughton
Oxfordshire	England	01865 333545	01865 333444	bhmarket@repp.co.uk	
	England	020 7333 4454	020 7222 4352	westward.lock@virgin.net	
Florida	USA			billt@softcell.org.co	
	USA			marketing@christy.co	
	England	020 7443 9000	020 7443 1000	JoeS@arrows.co.uk	
	England	020 8444 0808	020 8444 5000	Info@harryc.co.uk	
	England	020 7445 7000	020 7445 6000		
	England	020 8665 7766	020 8665 7000	sales@darkin.co.uk	
Midlothian	Scotland	0131 445 6800	0131 445 6236	scot@citypub.co.uk	
	England	020 8556 4354	020 8556 3030		
Herts	England			marketing@bpu.co.uk	
	England			info@ocp.ac.uk	
				karen@carl.co.uk	
	England	020 7334 3344	020 7334 2000	gill@trueform.co.uk	

Book table data

ISBN	Title	AuthorID	PublisherID	CategoryID	Row Number
014 032382 3	In & Out Stories	8	11	4	3
0 14 037022 5	Castaways	8	6	4	12
0 14 930654 7	The 2nd World War	3	14	14	1
0 15 056473 6	Teach Yourself Access	13	1	5	12
0 345 12342 3	Campfire Cooking	20	8	6	21
0 34532 375 1	Garden Shrubs	6	8	11	13
0 412 32132 2	African Drums	14	1	1	14
0 412 46512 1	Bits & Bytes	13	2	5	12
0 416 23765 3	West Highland Way	7	1	20	14
0 45 469861 2	Hamsters at Home	8	6	2	4
0 465 77654 3	Giant World Atlas	20	13	20	14
0 482 31456 1	Easy Internet	17	2	5	12
0 55345 456 2	The Night Sky	2	13	3	20
0 563 49124 5	Bread and Biscuits	11	7	6	21
0 576 26111 2	Crazy Comets	15	13	3	20
0 587 39561 0	Changing Skies	16	2	3	7
0 664 58123 4	Reading with the Under 5's	8	1	8	6
0 758 34512 1	Perfect Pizzas	11	15	6	21
0 85234 432 6	Outdoor Adventures	12	10	20	14
0 99988 452 1	The Tortoise in the Corner	4	6	4	12

Book table data (cont.)

Shelf Number	Number of copies	Publication year	Price	Reference	Lending	Picture
2	3	1987	£3.99	No	Yes	
2	2	2004	£4.50	No	Yes	
5	3	1988	£12.50	No	Yes	
3	2	2007	£8.99	No	Yes	
2	1	2005	£4.99	No	Yes	
2	2	1996	£4.99	No	Yes	
5	1	2002	£12.50	No	Yes	
3	2	2002	£9.99	No	Yes	
4	1	1982	£12.50	No	Yes	
2	1	2009	£4.50	No	Yes	
4	1	2001	£35.00	Yes	No	
2	2	2006	£9.99	No	Yes	
4	2	1991	£35.00	Yes	No	
3	2	1997	£12.50	No	Yes	
3	1	1989	£17.50	No	Yes	
5	2	2000	£10.99	No	Yes	
2	2	1991	£6.99	No	Yes	
5	2	2006	£9.99	No	Yes	
4	2	1985	£15.00	No	Yes	
3	2	1991	£6.50	No	Yes	

Category table data

Category Name
Adult Fiction
Animals
Astronomy
Children's Fiction
Computing
Cooking
Craft
Education
Family
Foreign Language
Gardening
Geography
Health
History
Music
Poetry
Religion
Romantic Fiction
Science
Travel

If you've mastered half of what's in this book, you are well on the way to becoming a proficient Access user. If you have got to grips with most of it, you are doing very well indeed.

You'll find lots of information on Access on the Internet, in addition to the local **Help** system.

You could also try searching the Web for sites that provide information on Access. Try entering "Microsoft Access" + "Software Reviews" into your search engine. You should come up with several sites worth a look.

If you would like to join a course to consolidate your skills, you could try your local college, or search the Internet for online courses. Most courses cost money, but you may find the odd free one – try searching for +Access +Tutorial +Free.

Good Access skills are useful on many different levels – personal, educational and vocational. Now that you have improved yours, why not consider going for certification? The challenge of an exam can be fun, and a recognized certificate may improve your job prospects. There are a number of different bodies that you could consider.

You may want to consider Microsoft Office Specialist (MOS) exams or ECDL (the European Computer Driving Licence – basic or advanced) certification. If you feel more ambitious, how about other Microsoft Certified Professional exams!

Visit **www.microsoft.com/learning/mcp/officespecialist/ default.mspx** for more on MOS certification or **www.ecdl.com.uk** for information on ECDL.

index